INSIGHTS FOR SEEKERS OF SELF

GREAT IS THY
FAITHFULNESS

OLIVE ROSE STEELE

Names have been changed, and details of incidents blurred to protect people's privacy
Scriptural translations are taken from the King James Version of the Bible

Copyright © 2010 Olive Rose Steele

All rights reserved

ISBN: 978-1475150629
Published in 2012
Great is Thy Faithfulness: Insights for Seekers of Self
Includes bibliographical references.

CONTENTS

Acknowledgments

Prologue by S.S.Laing, PhD

Introduction

PART ONE	My Journey, Your Journey, Our Journey	10
PART TWO	This Journey We Call Living	56
PART THREE	Our Faithful Deeds	103
PART FOUR	All Is Well	118
PART FIVE	Our Faithfulness	140
	Suggestions: 1-23	145
	Prayers	153
	Epilogue	168
	Parting Words	169

ACKNOWLEDGMENTS

Thank You, Heavenly Father, for assigning me the task of writing *Great is Thy Faithfulness*; this is an assignment unlike any You've called me to complete; thanks to my daughter, Dr. S.S.Laing for writing the Prologue; to my husband, for holding the mirror up to my face, every moment as he and I journey together; to Kathleen Daley and Shirley Campbell, for being such good friends; and to my readers for waiting patiently to read this Edition of my thoughts on Self. I acknowledge the Authors I cited in *Great is Thy Faithfulness*. Their inspired writings and teachings were divinely placed on my path to nourish my spiritual growth and development. Throughout *Great is thy Faithfulness,* I draw on true-life comparisons to link events in a common-sense yet humorous way. Be inspired!

PROLOGUE

Great is Thy Faithfulness is a pointed journey around the bends and through the curves and grooves of life that is skillfully captured using simple themes and enhanced through spiritual reflection. The author explores and shares the many themes from her life's journey—Ego, self-belief, respect, judgment, truth-telling, ambition, authenticity, change, stillness, and acceptance—mirror the range of emotions that we all encounter in our own life journey. However, her account is valuable because she helps us reflect on these life themes' source and purpose by simply calling them out, forcing a level of honesty that initially feels burdensome. She then allows us to lift the burden by offering prayer as the alternative to 'going it alone,' Surprisingly, we experience levity in the midst of hard truths. To fully experience *Great is Thy Faithfulness*, one must be still, open, and willing to be reflective; this is not a 'coffee-table' piece. As you read, you will find yourself revisiting a life circumstance, reflecting on your stance on a situation, re-evaluating your interpretation and approach to handling the situation, and re-organizing your experience. *Great is Thy Faithfulness* may ultimately help the reader achieve a level of honesty and acceptance about the "Is-ness" of life devoid of foreboding and rich in clarity and buoyancy.

S.S. Laing, Ph.D., Psychology

INTRODUCTION

I WAS ON A ROLLER coaster ride—descending fast. While clutching a slender rail, sweaty-palmed, in midair, enveloped in fear, I took stock of my unstable and vulnerable position and considered the possibility that a slight shift could land me on the ground with broken limbs or worse. In *Great is Thy Faithfulness,* I put forward the timid habits that debilitated my life progress; I identified my harmful lifestyle and Ego-based fears; and, without shilly-shallying, I stated my ruminations over lies I told myself about my precarious state of affairs. I wrote *Great is Thy Faithfulness* to complete my thoughts on Ego, true Self, and the incredible power of prayer. Our beliefs are mostly about our experiences, and so, when we pray, we sometimes express pessimism that does not support our goals—we obsess about our fears, and we dramatize our emotions. Many of us pray to maintain what we like about our Self and request more of what we want, need, and enjoy. Just as many embrace prosperity as a natural value to life, others accept spiritual wellness to maintain their sense of right and wrong. More of us are in search of spiritual renewal. We are seeking out answers to gut-wrenching soul questions. All are examining Self in a big way. Something inside of us keeps churning, stirring, seeking, and reaching for completion. We are using prayer as an additional spiritual tool to help us to withstand the trials of daily living.

In the stillness of our heart, we find the courage to approach the One we call Almighty to express praise. Souls are crying out for a personal relationship with God. We are living in a time of great miracles, wonders, modern innovations, and global developments. Spiritual observers are showing up as Preachers, Evangelists, Prophets, Imams, Healers, and others. Excitement is in the air. Readers of my book *And When We Pray* are familiar with my expression: Built-in Prayer Mechanism. I use a term as a reminder that I am, and everyone else is, predisposed to pray. Deep in our psyche is embedded our Built-in Prayer Mechanism, which stirs us, moment by moment, and leads us to pray.

In this Edition, I give insights and express my views on how one may navigate spiritual living's ups and downs. Wherever you stand in the present moment, whatever is occurring in your life, you should know that you are foremost the apple of God's eye (Lamentations 2:1-8) and therefore worthy of His faithfulness. The title *Great is Thy Faithfulness* is from the Book of Lamentations in the Holy Scriptures: *It is of the Lord's mercies that we are not consumed because his compassions fail not. They are new every morning: great is thy faithfulness* (Lamentations 3:22-23). I use God's male depiction throughout this Edition; however, I use the female characterization elsewhere. My female definition shows the parental emotions that I feel when I connect with the spirit within. Let us journey together on an exploration of Self in a way many are reluctant to pursue.

Olive Rose Steele
Ontario, Canada

PART ONE:

MY JOURNEY, YOUR JOURNEY

OUR JOURNEY

Same as how those who travel frequently are flexible about temporary detours and delays and will re-group in response to circumstances, those who travel the spiritual route must have faith that all will be well when an unscheduled diversion occurs.

IT IS TRENDY for people to describe specific periods of their life as *a journey,* and some people may stay on a particular journey for a reason. Notwithstanding, most people concede that life carries with it a plan for everyone, even if they believe they're in control of their destiny. People use influences, relationships, networks, and so on to successfully move their journey forward, although it is not unusual to journey with no real strategy. People might liken their journey to a ride in the family car. They see the advent of the GPS as god-sent, even if the GPS cannot match or replace the moment-by-moment directions that those who travel in a spiritual mindset will receive through divine know-how.

I see my journey as similar to being on a trip. Not like the trips I take when I visit a friend or a relative or go on a much-needed vacation.

My journey consists of steps through life that lead me to new and different places and unite me with traveling folks on the same path. My nonstop daily steps allow me to travel in an uninterrupted prayer atmosphere guided by a spiritual communication system described as a *Built-in Prayer Mechanism*. I talk about this Built-in Prayer Mechanism that in my book: *And When We Pray:*

"I take for granted that we are created with an instinct that lets us cry out in times of trouble to an unseen some "One," some "Thing" or some "Sense."

When we think about other people who never had and probably never will have access to a brand of spiritual doctrine, we may perceive them as unsophisticated individuals living in faraway places; even so, they are aware of the existence of a Higher Power as a way of life, they feel the presence of Spirit within, and they communicate and receive divine guidance during their sojourn here on earth. Everyone is created to connect with this Higher Power by looking within his own heart—it is what I call our Built-in Prayer Mechanism engaged. This mechanism propels folks to extend towards the mighty unseen One in their prayerful moments. I was deep under my duvet (my comforter), worrying over my sorry situation and sweating my prayers when the term *Built-in Prayer Mechanism* came into my heart. I always thought I had to know the right words to say and the correct format to employ if I was ever going to receive answers to my prayers, but to my surprise, I was pressed to be still and wait for my Built-in Prayer Mechanism to activate divine Spirit within. Our Built-in Prayer Mechanism might otherwise be called our Comforter; it stirs our faith and informs us of everything we need to know when we need to know. Our Built-in Prayer Mechanism is that spiritual system that allows us to reach out when the urge to pray presents itself. It comforts, directs, and guides us in our moments of communion with Spirit within. Our Built-in Prayer Mechanism raises our spirituality to a higher level; it is the part of us that makes the divine connection; extends our faith, and *stirs* us to say the right words for the right moment. How marvelous! This Built-in Prayer Mechanism that I talk about makes us have faith when our situations seem impossible. For example, the tumor is diagnosed as inoperable; your chances of conceiving are zero; your spouse reveals that it is time to call the marriage "a day" and wants a divorce; and your out-of-control child telephones from jail. What do you do? Be guided by your Built-in Prayer Mechanism as it prompts you to pray—trust the Divine to make your outcome positive. And when we don't understand or make sense of what is going on in our life, our Built-in Prayer Mechanism is that peaceful wind that lifts our spirit and reminds us that God is in our midst. As we give way to our Built-in Prayer Mechanism, our prayerful words pour out with ease as though we're talking to a friend rather than the all-powerful Master. When we are still, our Built-in Prayer Mechanism stirs the quiet place in our hearts.

The call to walk by faith, not by sight

"And I said to the man who stood at the gate of the year: 'Give me a light that I may tread safely into the unknown.' And he replied: 'Go out into the darkness and put your hand into the Hand of God. That shall be to you better than light and safer than a known way.' So I went forth, and finding the Hand of

God, trod gladly into the night. And He led me towards the hills and the breaking of day in the lone East."

—Minnie Louise Haskins, *The Gate of the Year*

I have heard various expressions of the word faith, and the one term that appeals to me best is, "Walk by faith, not by sight" (*2 Corinthians 5:7*). Whether sighted or not, most people would agree that walking without looking ahead could be frightening—people would prefer to see where they're heading rather than a leap of faith. The call to walk by faith, not by sight, becomes a major consequence for *control freaks* like me who may not be sure about the meaning of such a call; and faith the size of a mustard seed may be enough to move a mountain even if no one now living has that much faith. (*Matthew 17:20*). Let's acknowledge that having faith means having strong beliefs, and strong beliefs produce miracles; let's agree that everyone has faith. The difference is where people place their trust and what outcomes they would like to see manifested when they exercise faith. Traditions and cultures may rouse faith responses, and religious lectures to move people's consciousness and possibly generate questions like How may I integrate my walk by faith with my daily living? Will faith diminish my fears? What is my responsibility for other people's faith? Is my faith other people's business? Should the views of other people determine my faith? Same as how those who travel frequently are flexible about temporary detours and delays and will re-group in response to circumstances, those who travel the spiritual route must have faith that all will be well when an unscheduled diversion occurs. Not a day goes by that people are not met with advertisements, promotions, news broadcasts, media, and world affairs, designed to entice them into a lifestyle that requires their participation in a merry-go-round of activities. I put forward and support a spiritual approach to dealing with the issues of life.

My issues, your issues, we all have issues

The Scriptures encourage us to *Keep thy heart with all diligence; for out of it are the issues of life" (Proverbs 4:23)*

The issues of life, in my opinion, are a mixed bag of faith, hope, love, family, relationships, health, poverty, shortage, world affairs, and much more. And these are deep-seated issues that will pop up to scare, confuse, and distract. Many people are terrified that the issues in their personal lives will *swallow* or *bury* them. So the stress of navigating these issues invariably morph into the various faces of fear to challenge, even though some people show a façade that says all is well. Some people are not aware that most of the moment-by-moment activities that make their life uncomfortable are issues over which they have complete control; folks should know that nothing is the way it seems, and everything is subject to change.

By and large, people are optimistic about the direction they're heading. Folks believe that if they have a job, work hard at their job, play by moral and ethical rules and worship their way, they will withstand the weight of issues that *pop up* in their life. Folks who see other folks as having similar problems and are coping with their issues might show some understanding, but basically, people are concerned with their issues. Here are some signs that alert me when my life's issues are getting the better of me: my mouth goes dry, my ears get hot, my pulse races, my stomach flips over and over, and I become more anxious about handling my daily affairs. When I recognize these signs, I know that fear is raising its ugly head, and it is time to banish fear into nothingness where it belongs.

As we journey

Life's journey carries with it the signature, beauty, and mystery of each individual. All of us can navigate our steps as we walk. Some folks will leave action plans on the drawing boards of life; they are the folks with lots of things to do but have no finishing point. Other folks will complete their undertakings because they know that time will always be on their side. Whereas achievements and successes are celebrated when they occur, disappointments and bumps along the road should remind folks to slow down. Supposed obstacles are for learning and, unquestionably, formative experiences. These experiences inform knowledge and help us to overcome daily challenges. Even though our knowledge grows with each experience, difficult situations will not change overnight. We could run into people whose beliefs might not fit our mode or support our travel. It is worthwhile to build on relationships that back our goals and ambitions. Rainy days (disappointments, frustrations, hurts, and injuries) will continue to cause delays in our life; jealous, fear-based people will be on our travel route, and our new route may look a lot like the old route when we come upon rough terrains. Sounds familiar? I am suggesting a way that will uplift Self through love and peaceful interactions.

Where do we begin?

"We are beginning to see ourselves in a new perspective, to generations before and after us, to the earth, to each other, to God."
— Marianne Williamson, *Illuminata*

A beginning is a starting point, a place to grow out of or take off from, a spot from which one blasts off, a position from which one declares "ready, set, go"; a commencement. Physical connections by men and women usually are where the journey for most folks starts. It is incredible to think that after such connections, part of us lingered long enough to latch on to an egg for nourishment and growth, and we survived the growth process that later landed us into the arms of people who nurtured and loved us until we matured enough to live on our own. The preceding might be considered one-dimensional; all the same, learned men and women have already given appropriate biological explanations for where we begin. I can say I showed up here by the collaboration with two people I call mother and father. And the *born-again* aspect of life that folks embrace is adequately explained in the writings of sacred teachers, the philosophical thoughts of learned scholars, religious beliefs, lectures, books, pamphlets, etc.

Born-anew / born-again

It comes to mind that to be born-anew or born-again, people must die to worldly ways of doing their life. Die to fear; die to hate; die to jealousy; die to every negative thought, feeling, and action that they harbor and be born again to love; and those who have had the born-anew or born-again experience will grow in a new way. Born-anew or born-again individuals will rise from the horrible state of hate, jealousy, greed, lies, negativity, and every unloving way; and will be revitalized and armed with everything they need to proceed on their journey through life. They will use the **Love** word more often. Words like *hate, dislike, resent*; and phrases like, *Look what you've done to me, It is all your fault,* and *I can't stand you* will be replaced with *I love you.* **Love** word will become the key to their awakening. By adding the **Love** word in every statement, people who are born-anew or born again are acknowledging their love for Self and at the same time saluting love in other people. I am not saying enemy thoughts and feelings will disappear from the consciousness of folks or the issues of life will no longer challenge them; the scriptures say in John 14:26, after such an awakening: "But the Comforter, which is the Holy Ghost, whom the Father will send in my name, he will teach you all things."

Who or what is your comforter?

Underneath my twenty-year-old down-filled duvet is where I go to converse with God—my duvet dries my tears, and calms my concerns during long prayers, and hugs and comforts me in worrisome moments. Every negative feeling that I have, my friend the duvet shows the snot and tears—*she* knows the range of my emotions—her folds are my hideaway every time I feel unloved. I used to believe my duvet was my comforter because *she* loved me without conditions. But the Comforter that needs to be spoken about is the One whom the Father sends. That Comforter is with us at all times. That Comforter teaches us everything we need to know. (John 14:26) Who or what is your comforter? Your comforter is probably your spouse, a friend, a son, a daughter, the inside of your closet, a seat in the park, a strong drink—all have someone or something they call a comforter. For many, the awareness of the True Comforter is an awakening to a new beginning.

Take comfort from a new beginning

Every moment of living is an opportunity to begin again. Life allows individuals to create new beginnings, make several starts, and participate in numerous "ready, set, go" undertakings. Glen and Sonia have been engaged for a long time. Sonia desires to be Glen's wife. Glen wants to be the father of Sonia's baby—two different reasons for a new beginning. Glen and Sonia's challenge is which new beginning to accomplish first— the baby or the marriage. I say all new beginnings should be pursued and celebrated. Mona spent many months mulling over ways to turn her hobby craft into a money-making business. She established that securing a sales booth at the local mall would be practicable and profitable—a viable new beginning for Mona but one that might be frightening for some people. In-as-much-as new beginnings might lose charm; if our new beginnings are our choices, we likely will take full responsibility for the results. A new beginning might be seen as an opportunity to do a different thing or make a change. It is good to make new beginnings what we want them to be to benefit from them; create a new beginning today. Things you should remember: New beginnings bring hope. New beginnings should be your choices. Don't be reluctant to start over. Every opportunity to embark on a new beginning is a fresh start given to you by life. Make several starts and participate in as many "ready, set, go" undertakings as you wish. Celebrate your new beginnings.

Challenges on our journey

Dorothy's heart skipped a beat when her telephone rang around 1: 30 A.M. Before she said the required "Hello," she looked to see if there was a light in her son Rayon's room. The door was open, the room was dark, and Rayon was not home. Dorothy breathed a sigh of relief when she recognized the voice at the other end of the telephone to be that of Rayon. "Mom, I was arrested; come now." Up to that point, Dorothy blamed everything that went wrong in Rayon's young life on the break-up of her marriage and imminent divorce from her husband Eric—she must be strong for Rayon. It is true, some people's challenges might seem miniscule when compared to other people's challenges.

Nonetheless, folks see themselves as having a most horrendous experience when they're faced with their own trials and crosses. Know that challenges make us take responsibility for what may be happening in our moments. Challenges are worthwhile reminders for understanding the complexity of our true Self; challenges let us re-think big decisions, challenges strengthen our character, and challenges remind us to pray. Challenges were not put in our life to make us miserable. If you believe you were dealt a *bad* hand, *play* with it; your ability to emerge a winner is evidence that there is a divine plan in place to address the challenges of life. When I heard about Dorothy's separation from her husband, Eric, I was taken aback. As a family friend, I participated at their wedding, their son Rayon's birth and baptism, and I enjoyed numerous family gatherings with them. I was genuinely floored by the revelation that the family was splitting up. Here are some tips to remember when confronted by challenges: expect other people to challenge how you handle your challenges, don't be swayed by pity or other people's solutions and advice, trust God and Self with your challenges. In discussions leading up to their divorce, Eric proposed that his wife Dorothy and their son Rayon remained in the matrimonial home as a way of managing the family's financial affairs. Dorothy asked for my opinion on the matter. I told Dorothy that Eric's proposal seemed fair because Rayon would be close to his school, and she could continue to live rent and upkeep-free. My pity or advice did not sway Dorothy—she moved out of the matrimonial home when she found the right place for her. We will be challenged by those who disagree with the decisions we make or the ideas we cultivate, and we may be held back by the challenges we unintentionally create. It is useful when we move through our challenges with less impact. When we are level-headed in how we handle our challenges, we may dare our challengers to test our decisions—take your advice—only you *truly* know and experience your challenges. Rely on Spirit within, trust God and Self with your challenges. Your heart is your open book before your Heavenly Father; your lengthy conversations with Him are recorded by life. God knows about your challenges—pay attention to your heart. You know you are on the right track when other people want to learn more about your method of handling your challenges.

Life - an ever-changing scenario

On life's stage, the part folks play may change to reflect the ever-changing scenario. On cue, some folks may exit a picture, and other folks may enter. Folks may hear the unexpected "Cut" or the delightful "Action." The stage background may not always be as folks wish; they may or may not want to go with the flow. There will be happiness and sadness, sunny days, and heartbreaking moments. How folks view the scenario is how they identify what is happening and participate in the *performances*. When I last bumped into my 89-year-old friend Rosie, she jokingly mentioned her aches and pains and her weakening joints. I chuckled and told Rosie that aches and pains were "par for the course"—she would live to be one hundred notwithstanding her aches and pains and weakening joints. Before we parted, Rosie and I arranged to go for coffee after Church the following Sunday—to my surprise, Rosie expired before Sunday. Rosie's exit left me second-guessing how I maintain my social relationships. Was I too busy with personal activities to be socially attentive? Should my parting phrase: *See you next time* be more thoughtful since it is possible that there might not be the next time?

Travel on your path

One and all should know that life's travel is meant to be stress-free and flexible. The scriptures say in Psalms 55:22 "Cast thy burden upon the Lord, and He shall sustain thee." At the start of our journey through life, we trusted parents or guardians to nurture and maintain us during critical periods of our walk. But our outlook changed when we understood that we could travel independently on our path. We may journey on a spiritual path throughout all of the periods of our life, at our pace. We may journey during the spring and summer periods, or we may start a spiritual journey during the fall and winter periods—we decide when we are spiritually ready. We could meet individuals who may be more spiritually informed. They're the people who might teach us ways of walking in a spiritual mindset. We might bump into dishonest people, or we might bump into upright people—be constantly aware of your traveling companions and be ready to walk gingerly with them. We will come upon blind corners, forks in the road, and bumpy terrains (disappointments, illnesses, and losses), don't be sidetrack by these inconveniences—be ready to address them. Choose when you're spiritually prepared to travel. Chart your independent course. Go your own way.

The ideal way should be of peace, love, goodness, and our *brother's keeper*. But not all of us will want to show compassion or support others' needs or share our resources, or exchange information, even though we know that such acts are noble. Most people—spouses, adult children, relations, friends, best friends, colleagues, and strangers are on their life journey; they probably will not want to give up any more than the minimum amount of their time and resources to *anyone*. Our reaction to how we are treated in our moments of need is predicated on how other people treat us. For example, we might offer a friend a cup of coffee if the friend first offered us coffee, or we may respond with a compliment if we were first complimented. Life's travel may be less stressful if we recognize our journey as linked with other travelers because everyone, knowingly or unknowingly, plays a role in another person's life. If you are put off by how people respond to you in your times of need, keep in mind that all that's required of you is to give love to the occurring situations.

How do others identify you?

How we identify our Self is quite often different from how other people remember us. Generally, people are identified by their gender and given names. Additional identifications are attached, removed, or embellished as time goes by and as personal history dictates. People validate how other people identify their full names by assigning titles like Mr., Mrs., Ms., Sir, Madam, Dr., and so on. However, such designations are subject to other people's views and opinions. It is true; other people will try to diminish your titles and brush off your designations. Know that your titles and designations are your collectibles, be proud of them; however, all should crave to be identified as authentic.

Authentic individuals are willing to be themselves and be ready to express their true feelings. I admit it is not easy to maintain authenticity in society because people frown upon wholeness that appears to be self-righteous. Moreover, authentic people's dilemma is that their actions may be perceived as selfish or even wrong. Authentic people know that they allow other people the same courtesy when they do what they do the way they do it. People are authentic when they show up without a mask or a disguise. Being authentic is not "what you see is what you get," it is, somewhat, "what you see was not rehearsed"; it is aware of your true Self—no airs, no arrogance, and no conceits. Being authentic is not merely being real; for people's realities are associated with their frame of mind, their viewpoints stem from a variety of their own emotions. I say respect for other people's realism and quickly exit from situations that dispute other people's authenticity. Authenticity lets you *be*, without *being*.

What are your feelings about...?

This is how some folks begin a conversation when they seek our reactions, opinions, and ideas. I argue feelings are also burdens that some folks carry—illnesses, fears, etc. It surprised me to know that some folks shy away from expressing their true feelings because they believe expressed feelings may be a weakness. People sometimes say: *I keep my feelings bottled up inside.* I suggest that such a statement is not frank, for feelings bottled up inside could spurt out at any moment—that's the way feelings work. Decide how you would like to act in response to your feelings. A friend and I stopped at a coffee shop. I bought two vanilla coffees. My friend was horrified that I paid too much for the brew. To get value, she complained that the coffees were not bursting with vanilla aroma. She insisted on two replacement coffees. The waitress complied. Out of fear of being seen as passive, I yielded my authenticity to the situation by siding with my friend's uncalled-for behavior. What kind of game was I playing? In my heart, I knew that my friend had pushed the coffee incident out of control. I also knew it would be selfish of me not to be concerned about the kind of impression my friend and I would leave at the coffee shop, yet I played along with rules that did not match my truth. Like me, some folks play the "for a quiet life" game to appease a situation. Know that you've taken significant strides when your *yes* and your *no* are what you truly mean. Be authentic—tell the truth. Express true feelings. Show up without a mask or disguise. Your *yes* and your *no* should be real.

What is your truth?

Truth is what we express with confidence and conviction even though other folks may disagree; the truth is our responsibility to others' truth, the truth in word and action on one accord. My truth and my story are one. My truth is my life experiences, talents, energies, personal relationships that I form, and how I maintain my spiritual and physical well-being. What is your truth? Is your truth your way of living? Is your truth your life purpose, your commitment, and devotion? Maybe your truth is your ethics, your morals, and your standards. Your truth might be an accurate statement that you live by; your truth might be how you show up or what you're reflecting at the moment;

your truth might very well be your solemn oath to another person. Our truth is a reflection of our spiritual health. Here are some truths to believe in. The truth is, God is within every living existence. Our life displays our conscious and subconscious truths. We have all we need to express our truth. Seek out a position that supports your truth.

Be truthful in all aspects of your life, tell the truth about what is on your mind, how you feel, what is happening in your moment—tell the truth so that you may get help. When we are truthful, we can be trusted; we are that loved one, that friend, and that colleague who is not deceptive. People are sometimes less than honest, believing it is okay to tell half-truths to make other people happy. Untruths have consequences; untruths will backfire and hit us in the butt at an inconvenient moment. I encourage everyone to speak only when they know that what they're about to say is true. If we are hurting and we say we're okay, we're not telling the truth; never say *yes* if you meant *no*. Our memories are also part of our truth. People sometimes embellish their memories to improve their profile. If we make up stories, gloss over truths, and craft answers to fit questions, we are not truthful.

It's about Ego / Self

"The Ego is the part of your mind that differentiates 'you' from 'everything else.' As such, it is a vital part of the technology of thought. It is that part that can conceive not only of thought but of the thinker of the thought." — Neale Donald Walsch, *When Everything Changes, Change Everything.*

You've probably seen depictions of the two pixies—one on each shoulder—showing the good side and the selfish side of humans. I make the correlation that one pixie is the Ego (selfish), and the other pixie is the true Self (loving). Ego is all about itself: me, myself, and I; Ego is insecure, it is in love with itself only, it demands admiration and keeps true Self fearful so that true Self will come back for stimulus; Ego is a companion for life, it never gives up on its mission to control true Self; Ego's desire is to divide and conquer to maintain its influence over true Self; Ego promotes itself as real because it believes it is our true personality, our true character; the truth is, we develop and expand our Ego as we grow and mature in our environments; Ego sees a motionless position as passive and it encourages us to show we are in charge; Ego insists that we hold our stance and pushes us to take what is ours if we felt we were deceived; Ego will appear in different ways, wearing different masks, to distract us; Ego continually reminds us of our importance and it will appear in every form imaginable to jog our memory about who we believe we are, this is our Ego's way of maintaining self-interest; Ego is arrogant, it makes us take notice of our status and some of us exert our privilege standing by squashing and dishonoring the status and talents of other people; Ego lets us believe we are the sum total of our lineage, our beliefs, our achievements, and our possessions. Ego affects us in significant ways, small ways, strong ways, weak ways, overpowering ways, and so on. And, left unrestrained, Ego will imitate other people's bad behaviors and lifestyles. Because Ego is all about itself, it has to be taught that it can love and give.

On the other hand, true Self is love on display. True Self is our personality, our character. True Self is ethical, moral, honest, and decent. True Self demonstrates love without any strings attached. True Self gives without counting the costs. True Self trusts itself. True Self is loving and giving.

When true Self shows Ego how to love, Ego recoils and is born again to love. At that moment, the Ego's plan to divide and conquer is no longer relevant. Remember this: true Self is the loving side of Ego, true Self treats Ego with love and kindness, Ego will cease to be a factor when love shows up because the mission of true Self is to teach Ego how to love.

Our ambition is related to our Ego

People will try to *make* something of themselves—have ambition, as they say, and some folks may observe others as having no ambition. Right now, I would like to apologize to those folks whom I told, to their faces, that they have no ambition; I was wrong. Our ambition is related to our Ego, and that is not a bad thing, for how else would we pursue our desires and dreams if we did not have the Ego to propel our ambition? Our ambition is our hopes and dreams, desires, and goals; God created us with an abundance of ambition. Ambition encourages folks to set goals, make plans, have desires, compete, and be proud if they so wish. Ambition makes people reach higher education; bigger jobs; weightier possessions; and more of the things that call attention to Ego. Know that as folks compete and go all-out for more, they might stir jealousy and resentment in the heart of other people's egos. If folks fib or fabricate to legitimize their ambitious Ego, those fibs could embarrass them later. Be honest, avoid damage to the true Self. Remember this: your ambition propels you toward your hopes, dreams, desires, and goals; your ambition encourages you to make plans, compete and be proud; your ambition makes you want to do your utmost; your ambition makes you want to go higher; be honest about your ambition, avoid damage to your true Self.

The ego will appear in different forms and sizes

The ego will appear in different forms and sizes, wearing multiple masks to deceive by giving the impression we are standing up for our Self. My Ego says I am or could be someone of consequence and importance. My Ego lets me identify other people's Ego as weak and pounce to show superiority. My Ego allows me to criticize relationships that appear threatening. My Ego pushes me to draw other people's attention to my accomplishments and possessions. My Ego insists that I command my world to stand up and take notice of me. In other words, everything about my Ego is for my self-importance. Such lofty thinking brings me back to reality very quickly and reminds me that my place is not of dominance but service and humility.

Let's look at the Ego as overpowering. Overpowering Egos highlight shortcomings in other people. Overpowering Egos manipulate lesser Egos to do it's bidding. Overpowering Egos are unwilling to see good in others. Overpowering Egos pretend to love. We must know our true Self, to be able to stand up to an Ego that wants to overpower us. I deal with such an Ego by refusing to accommodate it. How? When an Ego shows up as overpowering, I call it by its name and send it back into nothingness, where it belongs, meaning I treat the overpowering Ego with *cautious* love. Is an overpowering Ego all that bad? No. An overpowering Ego is indicating a struggle through the challenges of life's competitive journey. The overpowering Ego may be seeking to address some issues of life that it faces—here is where true Self treats the overpowering Ego with (cautious) love. Let us look at Ego appearing in a spiteful mask.

Eula's Christmas gift to me was a beautiful gray leather jacket that she purchased while on vacation in London, England, many years earlier. The detailed topstitch, the extraordinarily-shaped silver buttons, and the well-placed panel in the center back are classy features. Over the years, I secretly wish to own a similar jacket. So when I opened my gift the Christmas in question and saw the jacket, I concluded that my aunt knew all along that I *had my eyes* on her jacket. One evening I wore my gray leather jacket to a diner and hung it in the coatroom. Later that evening, I noticed it was missing. I was beside myself. My spiteful Ego took over my senses, and I vowed that if I did not find my gray leather jacket, I would make it my mission to grab one of equal value. A short time later, I attended a concert and saw a black leather jacket (not nearly as rare as the one given to me by my Aunt Eula, although the buttons were uncommon and the leather was soft and supple) hanging in the coatroom. "What's good for the goose is good for the ..." I said and walked out with the jacket.

Vindications, in any moment, may seem reasonable and may give some folks a temporary feeling of satisfaction; however, I could not claim an item that did not belong to me even though my Ego applauded. I returned the jacket to the theater and posted a notice in my local newspaper's lost-and-found pages. My point? People may find it challenging to think loving thoughts when Ego screams for revenge. And those who take revenge may believe they're doing what's right or standing up for themselves. They may believe that if no one witnessed the offense, the bad behavior wouldn't matter. Be alert to an Ego that pops up wearing a spiteful mask—quash it quickly. The item may be an inexpensive pair of sunglasses, hand them over, someone will thank you without your even knowing.

Eyes are always watching

As we journey, eyes watch and observe. Other eyes notice our travel gear, the company we travel with, the things we carry, and our accumulated successes along the way. If we appear to be successful, other travelers may want to join our company. Some people and some things stay with us for a long time (a spouse, children, family, good friends, positions, possessions, etc.) and so if, or perhaps when, a child requests independence, a friend moves far away, and a valued position is replaced, folks may feel rejected. Know that the players come and go; you have to believe you can survive a fearful change; do the best you can to make it through difficult or challenging periods, by faith, help is available. It is not unusual for people, situations, and things that no longer serve to exit or conclude. This was true for me when I lost my job. I admit the decision to fire me was necessary because I was no longer an asset to my employer; I was an employee to be rid of. Know that it is not alright to hold back your journey or put your travel in jeopardy just because you believe you're responsible for advancing another person's life plans, there is much for you to do along the way, and your travel should not be hindered. There may be times when other people's decisions impact your flow, understand that not in all cases will you make your own crucial decisions; other people will make decisions that might not be positive for you. In those moments, when another person's decision interrupts your flow, know that you can take a stand; it is not alright to put your journey in jeopardy to satisfy other people. Remember, your life ebbs and flows in your direction.

Be clear about your lines of demarcation

"R-e-s-p-e-c-t, find out what it means to me."
—*Song composed by Otis Redding*

Folks who say they're *only human* are saying: *I want to do as I please, don't make me responsible for my conduct*; they're the folks who believe it is alright to be impolite. Folks will follow set rules and show a measure of politeness as the maximum amount of respect they are prepared to give. Regardless, most people try to be respectful. What is your meaning of respect? What are some rules that guide how you show respect? What do you expect from others as a proper response to your show of respect to them? Do you respect other people's fundamental right to live happy, healthy, and whole? Matt, head of IT, was rather self-important in his presentations until a co-worker disagreed with a remark he made. Matt was annoyed. He expressed his displeasure—not because he thought the co-worker was uninformed but because the co worker's observations embarrassed him. Folks who cross a demarcation line at an inappropriate moment to advance an opinion might disrupt another person's flow.

Do you create drama to gain respect? Do you make yourself indispensable to get respect? Do you earn respect by your actions and your money? Do you always want a *thank you* note as a sign of respect? If you answered yes to any of the above questions, you are not alone. All of us—you and I, want people to show us recognition, respect, if you will, for the things we should have been doing anyway. Respect will come easier when we treat other people how we want to be treated and acknowledge them as equals. Respect will return to folks who respect themselves. My creed is: play by moral and ethical rules, avoid being contemptuous to fellow life travelers and try to be polite under all circumstances, right here, right now. Established limits may bring folks some respect, although it is possible that other folks could find ways to enter into areas where they have no business. Some people reason that they know what's right for everyone. The key is to be clear about your lines of demarcation. Remember this: a show of respect acknowledges that all are equal; it is possible to show respect for others under all conditions, right here, right now; set boundaries, guard your space, be clear about your line of demarcation; where there are no boundaries, other people might set one without your approval; don't cross other people's boundaries. R-e-s-p-e-c-t, what does it mean to you?

Dear God
Lord and Father of all
Teach me to be respectful of other people
To be respectful of their traditions
To be respectful of their worship and praise
To be respectful of their language
To be respectful of their right to be different
To be respectful of your Divine Spirit
Within each and every one of Your children
And help me to be respectful of myself before
I ask other people to be respectful of me
In Jesus Name
Amen.
(And When We Pray)

Prayer—your ongoing conversation with God

When you pray, you're performing a natural act of expressing your heart's desires with faith in the Invisible Force that sustains life, to deliver that for which you prayed. Why you pray, how you pray, and when you pray are determined by your understanding of the Spirit within and the role God plays in your life. There will be times when you will not find words to express yourself—God knows what is in your heart, and He will answer your prayerful thoughts. Prayer is what you should rely on for your every need. Prayer should be your ongoing conversations with God—it is what you ought to do because you are alive. Your prayerful conversations are between you and God. Some of us were taught to pray by our parents or guardians as part of a tradition; others learned to pray in places of worship. Still, others learned to pray on their own due to situations that forced them to plead. Whether you were taught at an early age or learned this rite later as you mature, or, like so many people, circumstances propelled you to speak your heart to comfort your soul, sooner or later all express themselves in prayerful ways. People pray for calm and inner peace, family and friends, receive miracles, fulfill spiritual obligations, and assuage fear. My reasons for praying is all of the above. I can testify that my prayers reduce my worries and negative emotions and make me feel love for my Self and others. When you're faced with an unpleasant situation and deem it necessary to pray, go deep—surrender your fears, and yield to your Built-in Prayer Mechanism. I encourage people to rely on the tremendous power of their prayers. I say *feel* your emotions when you pray, then rest the situation in God's hand; A simple prayer is all that is needed because God already knows what is in your heart. Some people will be skeptical of such statements. If you accept that prayer is a continuous, 24/7 activity, then you might wake up some mornings reciting your prayers. The awesome power of your prayers is what you ought to rely on. It is the sure way to remain centered and be able to endure challenging moments. Irrespective of your approach, whether you plead your cause or give over your occurring situations to others to plead on your behalf, prayer should be regarded as a sacred act that calls for divine approach. In moments of distress and dire need, you will be prompted to express yourself prayerfully. In other words, all of us—you and I—have a built-in system of communication that can and should be stirred. To my advantage, I developed a prayer-on-the-run approach to ease my fear-based circumstances. In my moments of confusion, the short recitals of "Lord have mercy," "Oh my God," or "Help me, Jesus," were all I thought I needed. Those quick prayers gave me the feeling that I was in control of what was occurring and the illusion that my spirituality was intact. But the times when I found myself up to my knees in my fear-based mess, understanding how I got into such situations was a challenge in itself. In those times, I sought longer prayerful conversations with God, as I call on my Built-in Prayer Mechanism to guide me. Our prayers are our connection to the One we call Almighty. Know that when you pray, the Spirit world listens. Are you surprised when someone tells you that something happened to them, which answers their prayer? We—you and I—are used by a Higher Power, every moment to deliver the answers to other people's prayers. Rely on the awesome power of your prayer, trust in your prayer for your every need, prayer is what you ought to do because you are alive, know that a host of angels are standing by, waiting to deliver your requests.

The awesome power of your prayers

Individuals who pray regularly will testify that prayers increased their ability to feel compassion for other people, prevented or even reversed sickness and disease, and improved their relationships and mental health. My focus of prayer is on maintaining a positive outlook, being truthful to my Self, setting worthwhile goals, and maintaining loving relationships.

Those who pray regularly can testify about their positive benefits. In times of distress, call on the awesome power of your prayers to heal your broken heart, to right a terrible wrong, to make straight a crooked way. Call on the awesome power of your prayers for strength on behalf of your family and friends, call on the awesome power of your prayers when you are short of funds or in a financial bind, call on your prayers for miracles, call on your prayers for perfect health.

Mrs. Ball was a praying woman. She led a vibrant prayer group in her Church. When Mrs. Ball's husband became ill, her prayer group was in constant prayer for Mr. Ball's healing. Mr. Ball recovered fully and then *took off* with a member of Mrs. Ball's prayer group and never came back. My point is, some people will say they've prayed their hearts out, and yet their prayers have gone unanswered. I say pay attention to your prayers; you may have overlooked an answered prayer. Be alert.

And when your prayers frustrate you?

Some people have difficulty believing their supplications to be how they achieve divine balance, and so they don't trust their prayer requests to manifest as they desire; they tend to rely on the prayers of Priests, Pastors, prayer partners, and prayer groups to augment their spirituality, and that is a good thing because the prayers of righteous individuals are beneficial and where more than one are gathered in His name God is in the midst to bless. I grew up believing that if I was not a member of a specific religion if I did not openly confess my sins—too numerous to remember—and if I were not immersed in a baptismal custom (the choice of others), my prayers would not be manifested. My prayers were typically about me, my welfare, and the things that were important to me. I prayed to receive money in large amounts to purchase beautiful things; I prayed that situations I did not like would be averted; I prayed for the success of my family; I prayed for the success of my friends and, to be honest, I have prayed hurtful prayers if I thought someone offended me. And when some prayers discouraged me, I cried heavy, pitiful tears. There were times when (without rhyme or reason) I asked God to replace the things I broke. The idea that tears, as we pray, are the key to divine attention is misguided. When we lose something, break things, and ruin things is when we're not paying attention to our prayerful words. If praying frustrates you, if you feel that you have to pray through pitiful heavy tears, if you have to stomp your feet, if you are motivated to blame everyone for your misfortunes, if you feel that you have to stop praying in protest, then you know it is time to pay attention to your thoughts. Folks may be so absorbed with crying when they pray that they fail to recognize their answered prayers. Your supplications go where you send them; always rely on the awesome power of your prayers; your prayers are your connection to the divine Spirit. Be grateful for all the things you already have, be mindful that God is in the midst of your prayerful moments to bless. Believe in your supplications.

What is your prayerful approach?

In general, our prayerful approach is about how we feel at the moment. And because we are perfectly created, nothing is wrong with the way we approach prayerfully, in any given moment, in any setting, under any condition. Everything we say and do is as it should be. Our prayerful approach is our personality, our style. It appears to me like some people view their prayerful approach from a *self-ish* standpoint. A self-ish approach is a mindset of *my way or the highway*—meaning some folks are on the right track spiritually, and other folks are on the wrong track. Such an approach might make the *right track* people divine to the point where their primary goal is a crusade that calls for the *wrong track* people to repent of untold sins and be baptized in a specific manner before they might approach their Heavenly Father in prayer. People pray in houses of worship, on bended knees, with bowed heads; in a dark room; at the side of their bed; in groups; silently and out loud; use your style to advance your prayerful approach. My approach is simple—I express my feelings in prayer without requesting perfect answers with faith that my needs will be met in due course. Know that if you are *hung-up* about when, where, and how you approach, you probably will not recognize your answered prayers.

See a clear path

"I can see clearly now, the rain is gone/ I can see all obstacles in my way/ Gone are the dark clouds/ it's gonna be a bright (bright) sun-shiny day."
—*Song composed by Johnny Nash*

Foggy weather gives me the willies. I admit it is never exciting for me to drive my car on a day when I can see no further than the hood. I make the same comparison when I observe my life journey as spiritually foggy, and I usually praise as my mental visualization becomes clearer. But for their dedication and commitment to family, jobs, a crucial appointment, or a serious emergency, many people would rather not drive in foggy weather. Foggy weather or not, dedicated people will show loyalty even if their belief could change under different circumstances. As folks see their life journey more clearly, dedication to a line of business, a specific profession, or a cause may no longer be the most important activity for them.

There was a time when I dedicated my life to the family, but as my family matured and my ambition evolved, I became excited about advancing my passion—my purpose, if you will. The folks who see clearly reward Self with loving words and unselfishly dedicate time to Self by doing the things they enjoy. I encourage individuals to praise Self when a plan comes together and feel good about Self without prodding from others. People feel good about themselves when they set aside times for worshiping, praying, fasting, and meditating; they eat well, play often, sing and dance; they socialize with like-minded people, and give what they can afford. I love to pray, laugh, dance, and write—those things make me say, "aaaahh." You, too, have things you love to do that will make you say, "aaaahh." For example, praying is a daily spiritual activity that will make you see clearly and inspire other spiritual acts. A leisurely walk in the park could turn into an occasion to seek mercy; a day at the spa could also be a day of reflection and meditation, and time spent driving along a country road could be an occasion to observe the wonders of nature. Some situations that challenge our perspectives tend to make us see fog and tend to shift gears or go into reverse. I say, navigate carefully through your foggy weather—the fog will eventually wear off. Spiritual practices improve your eyesight and your mental function. On a clear day, I love to go mall hopping.

My husband no longer asks me, "Where are you off to?" He asks, "Which of the malls are you off to?" You may not relish mall hopping—no matter, do, and enjoy the things you like, dedicate to those things if you so desire. Clarity is a spiritual act of faith, practicing spiritual clearness, meaning setting aside time for worship, fasting, praying, and meditating. Commit time to social mingle in a church community of your choice; these activities can be easily integrated into your routine. You will agree with me that some of us spend too much time turning our life's journey into a full-time job—all work. There is more to life than working to pay the bills. Life should be an enjoyable game, and games were meant to be played. Have fun at the game of life—play your game with love. See clearly!

"Gone are the dark clouds that had me down /It's gonna be a bright (bright) sun-shiny day."
—*Song composed by Johnny Nash*

It might not be your "business."

Our journey is our *business*. Our responsibility is to our *business*, although the *business* of our friends and our relations may seep in and become relevant—we ought to take care of our own *business*. Everyone should know that their spouse's *business* and their adult children's *business* may not be their *business*. It is true, other people will do things that may not be to our liking, or they may not perform to our approval—the world may not be turning in their favor at that moment. Your journey is as you like it—difficult and full of challenges and drama, or uncomplicated and straightforward. Be cautious about taking on other people's *business*. See other people's *business* as issues for their attention. Other people's *business* will hold you back. Other people's fears are not your *business*. Your life's journey is your *business*. Always tread carefully around other people's business for other people's business (issues) could hinder your progress and hold you back. Be leery; you could end up accepting blame or be liable for decisions that were not your business. Principled individuals such as Priests, Pastors, Imams, and other spiritual mentors are always at hand to support your spiritual walk. If their counseling is not sufficient, other professionals might assist folks in handling their business. I say, look for good in all situations and accept what is acceptable to you—you do not have to be involved in other people's business. Remember, all of us are traveling with our own *business*; take care of your *business*.

A quiet feeling

"Whatever project you undertake, whether personal or business, spiritual or physical, noble or mundane, if you do not begin it from a mindful posture—from a quiet state of your being—you are headed for disappointment and failure. It's the nature of things." —David Kuntz, *Quiet Mind*.

Onlookers might find our quiet ways worrying. People who notice our calm behavior may express concerns about our happiness. But our quiet habit should be our way of connecting with the divine Spirit within. Quiet should be when we listen to what is in our hearts. Embrace quietness. Let's think about the hundreds of patrons that occupy a shopping mall on a given day, pay attention to the sounds you hear. Pretty quiet right? Yet malls are busy places. You could say malls are places of quiet activity—an odd kind of quiet. My point is—quiet symbolizes life. Quiet does not mean we don't utter a word or move an inch. Quiet is truly more than behaving a certain way. When we're quiet, we're allowing our spirit to develop a focal point. We're permitting our soul to connect on a higher plane, and we're making way for miracles to happen. Quiet is our time to listen. Quiet is when we hear what we're saying to our Self. It is when we receive answers to questions from the heart. In those moments of quiet, God's awesome power is working. We're not idle when we're exercising quietness because quiet moments are when our Built-in Prayer Mechanism is at work, leading and directing us in prayer. We will receive directions in our quiet state, answers will come, and we will emerge renewed and informed. Knowledge and information will come in spoken and written words to guide us along. Teachers will appear as needed to teach new lessons, instructors will show up to coach a new strategy, and mentors will present themselves to give counsel as required. The quiet of our heart is where we discover our authentic Self. In the quiet of our heart we recognize the divine Spirit within. Quiet assures that everything will turn out all right. The state of quiet is an additional spiritual tool—be quiet in meditation. Remember, in quietness: You're not idle. Quiet is your time to listen. You hear your true Self. You receive directions and answers. You experience peace. You're clearing the way for miracles. You're connected to the divine Spirit within.

False Quiet

The ego will suggest false periods of quietness such as soundless temper tantrums—times when you are unloving to others, the silent treatments you give to your spouse for reasons only known to you, the "my lips are sealed" stance you take when your opinion is required, and the "I don't care" responses you give when you disapprove of a decision. I have gone into my periods of fake quietness followed by bursts of Ego-based open rage. What are your reasons for being quiet? Are you not connecting with Spirit within? Would you like to make a statement, but words are eluding you? Is something wrong that only you can fix? Is your quiet simmering, just waiting to boil over? Regardless of what may be happening in your life, give yourself some quiet time to erase negative thoughts. Words might not be necessary at that moment; being at a loss for words is a good thing. Experience quiet in your special place as you hum the lyrics of songs you thought you had forgotten. Stay a while in the silence of your heart.

Discover for yourself how quiet you can be

"I'm convinced one of the reasons we enjoy it so much once we begin to spend time alone and quiet is that it encourages us to take life on its terms and make the best of it."
—David Kuntz, *Quiet Mind*

I was sitting in my office one afternoon, wrapped up in quiet contemplation, overwhelmed with thoughts about how I might adequately fund my company's next payroll—totally absorbed in my calamity. I made out that my eyes were closed, and my hands were prayerfully clasped. Out of the blue, I felt a distinguishable breeze blowing through my office, the sensation may have lasted just seconds, but the experience shook the chair in which I sat. I opened my eyes and established that my surroundings were still intact. At that moment, I was prompted to telephone my best client. "I am lagging with this week's payroll—may I collect your outstanding invoice today?" I said to him. "Sure," was the reply. Quiet allows folks to enter deep into their place of sanctuary to observe the practice of prayer and meditation, knowing that they need look no further for answers and solutions. At that place, everyone can yield in complete surrender. In that moment of quietness, everyone can discover that their world is in sync and revolving in their favor. The more we practice silence is, the more we will be spiritually informed. In quietness, everyone can experience the mighty power of the divine Spirit within. In stillness, we know what to do when challenges confront us. It is not easy to chase away negative thoughts that come in succession during quietness. It is hard to be quiet when the bill collectors call and harder still if we are jobless, homeless, friendless, and feeling no use whatsoever to ourselves or others. We live in a visual world. What we see is what we accept as true. But consider this: in our most challenging moment, our moment of adversity, we can be quiet, we can inhale several deep breaths to calm our worries; we can feel our heartbeat and know that the divine Spirit is our comfort within. Don't let noises, lack of personal comfort, or disturbances interrupt your quiet moments. Be quiet and know that the divine Spirit within is the power you already have and is all the power you will ever need. Be quiet and embrace Spirit in soundless space. Be quiet and *know*. Know that all is well, even though there will be times when what you seek is not what you get. The songs say: "There is a place of quiet rest, near to the heart of God."

–*Composer Cleland McAfee*

Quiet lets you experience the mighty power of Spirit within. Quiet invites prayer. Inhale several deep breaths and be quiet. Your quiet world is your place of rest.

Mother's quiet rest

Three years ago, I was put through a true-to-life test. My mother lay dying in her hospital bed. I lost my senses. I did not know whether I was going or coming, if I was praying or sweating, whether my Built-in Prayer Mechanism was still accessible, or God had abandoned me. I was scared. I admit I am selfish. I wanted my mother to live forever, but I was prepared to pray heaven down for mother to live longer since that was not possible. At 83 years old, I honestly thought my mother was too young to die. Like me, you will feel your parents too young to die, no matter the age at which they make their exit. I was not ready to concede the death of my mother. So I bent over mother, my face close to her face, my warm breath bounced off her face and back on to mine, my pulse raced, both my ears were hot, and my stomach flipped over and over. Fear of losing my mother to death set in—I would never see her again, hear her laugh again, listen to her call my name again—I was petrified. My ears were scorching. I prayed:

Dear God
In the name of Jesus Christ, heal my mother
Make her whole again
Give my mother three more years of life
Father, You know that I am not yet ready to let her go
I cannot live without her in my world
Have mercy upon my mother and
Extend her life for my sake.
(Olive Rose Steele)

I looked away from my mother to dry my eyes, and when I looked back at her, she had taken flight. Mother's departure from this life was not about me; it was about mother and God. My mother was ready to enter the Promised Land, where the angels and all of her friends and loved ones, including her parents and my guardian angel (mother's grandmother), were waiting to welcome her home. Looking back, I did not lose my senses, for my Built-in Prayer Mechanism was within, waiting to be accessed, and my Heavenly Father did not abandon me. Events come about to remind us of certain inevitabilities. The sooner we learn to accept these events as occurrences that we cannot avoid or change, the healthier and more bearable our journey will be. People will deal with the departure of loved ones by observing respectful periods of mourning, and most folks will move on with their lives as quickly as possible, mainly to assuage their fears. What is your intention when you pray? Is your intention to experience a personal moment of communion with your divine Heavenly Father? A self-serving request to turn a situation in your favor for your sake? Is your prayer a gut-wrenching demand for revenge? Seriously, why do you pray? Every prayer request resounds on a higher plane—be serious when you pray. Prayer is a 24/7 activity that will keep you linked to Spirit within. Pray always.

PART TWO:

THIS JOURNEY WE CALL LIVING

Living makes us fearful in situations over which we have no control—the fear of world wars, devastating earthquakes, hurricanes, floods, thunderstorms, and a prophetic doomsday are fears that make folks tremble.

LOVING, LAUGHING, CRYING, fearing, and dying makes our journey the well-rounded package we call life. We say we love life, yet we fear the unknown aspects that accompany life. We would prefer not to experience the challenges that life has in store for us.

Why?

Because we fear.

Fear is a typical response to a life-changing situation, a strange occurrence, or a new test. Fear is our first reaction when we face the unknown or an enemy. Fear is the thing that makes people cringe in moments when they're required to stand up. Fear is the thought that makes one's stomach turn over, knowing that she must face an edgy conclusion, such as the passing of a loved one, the rejection of a spouse, or the significance of a diagnosis. Fear is dread. We fear because we identify things that happen in our life as good and evil. Fear of evil terrifies dreadfully, evil breaks trust, evil encourages malice and spite—fear no evil. (*Psalms 23:4*). Evil is a phony fear that might *take* root in a mind that's starved for self-confidence. Fear of evil makes evil seem real. No matter what is happening in your moment, it will negatively overwhelm your thinking if you believe it to be evil. Know that doubt and fear are companions; they operate in unison to challenge the perception of goodness. Banish fear of evil, banish doubt and anxiety.

What are your dreaded fears?

Do you fear you may become very successful in your endeavors? Do you fear you may reach a level of attainment which you will not be able to sustain? Do you fear the riches for which you yearn will materialize, and you will enjoy more comfort than you truly deserve? Do you fear you could receive your heart's desire, thereby attracting unwanted attention? Do you fear you could receive the love you cannot reciprocate? Do you fear you might be vulnerable to other people's inflicted evil? Do you fear there might be someone "out there" who might want to harm you for no good reason? All of us have dreaded fears. People talk about incidents that are not to their liking as their worst fears. These fears will terrify me the same way that my fear of poverty terrifies me.

My fear of poverty

Poverty is the one fear that makes me tremble. The thought of being poor brings instant tears to my eyes. In my mind, there is really no misery like poverty. Poverty denotes a shortage; a yearning to have more; a desire for things that are out of one's reach; scarcity of love and affection; poverty diminishes one's association with family and friends; poverty causes a man and a woman to feel less of a person; poverty fosters lack of faith in a brighter future. Poverty is a curse! It sucks to be poor! I struggled with the fear of poverty, fear of loss of credibility, fear of loss of love, fear of people I call enemies, and fear of the unknown. One or more of these fears hindered me at different stages of my life.

Coupled with these fears were my equally empty, fearful prayers. My worries are not different from yours, my friends; we share some of the same concerns. Operating funds *dried up* fast. I was devastated. My business was not yet equipped to function on its own I did not acquire all the toys I wanted to play with. I became angry. I was too preoccupied with my selfish Ego to recognize the part I played in the company's weakened position. The fear of poverty set in. I felt I was never going to be the prosperous individual I wanted to be. All of the so-called failures I ever experienced flashed back as reminders of meager times. God had abandoned me. My entire psyche went into fear mode: fear of losing credibility, fear of failure, fear of being called a failure, fear of rejection, fear of loss of love, fear of not being good enough, fear of fear itself. I was a walking, talking fear package. If you admit to any of the fears I mentioned above, you're conceding that you *are* not because you *have* not, and that's a lie the Ego tells to keep folks angry. We fear because we forget that nothing is as it looks; things and situations are the way they should be because that's the way life is. We are happy when things are going well and fearful when things are not to our liking. Poverty is a mask that fear wears to disguise and scare the Self. Don't ever say—*I am poor*—say—*everything I need, I have.* Poverty is a lie. I suggest that folks acknowledge the impartiality of life and identify the state of poverty as it genuinely is—nothing.

When fear raises its ugly head

My business had been struggling to stay afloat, rent and upkeep were three months past due, significant decisions regarding the life of the company had to be made, and the office was slated to be vacated. It was a crisp, chilly, late December morning. I fell asleep the night before in a confused, perplexed, and fearful frame of mind—the impending eviction gnawed me the entire night. I woke up in the same state of anxiety that put me to sleep and considered I could remain in that state of confusion for as long as I desired, or I could banish my fretfulness and set my mind at ease. I could not make up my mind whether to see a therapist, run away, and be absent for a long time or advise my husband to commit me to the insane asylum. (We will indeed devise selfish ways of handling our crisis in ways that some may call crazy.) I was experiencing a roller-coaster moment. Hate and resentment had taken over my senses. The situation that had been bothering me was very hurtful. When I am vexed, I temporarily lose my hearing and barely see, let alone focus. But I surrendered every negative thought I harbored at that moment and turned to Self to see me through. On the December morning, I jogged to my quiet place—the place where I go to commune with Spirit. (Your quiet place maybe your private moment in your heart).

I sat on a large rock overlooking the river below. In the stillness of the moment, I closed my eyes and contemplated the sound of my beating heart. I marveled at the life-giving substance that was flowing through my veins. I inhaled several deep breaths. With my Built-in Prayer Mechanism in motion, I prayed. As I prayed, I released my mind to forgive and be forgiven. When I opened my eyes and looked around, the scenery was different; rays from the morning sun bounced off the nearby mound, and birds perched in quiet clusters in observance of the moment. At that moment, I knew I was part of a creation that needed my presence.

I knew all that was required of me was to be still and be relevant. At that moment, I knew there was no need to fear. I recognized the moment that required me to forgive. I needed to truly forgive myself for every negative thought and action that led me to the fear I experienced, and I most definitely had to forgive everyone who played a role in my fear. So, I excused myself for being angry for so long; I recognized that the hurt I felt was a combination of my worries and mattered to no one but me—it made no difference to my landlord or the bailiff who locked my office. I accepted my circumstances due to decisions I had made, and I forgave the folks I believed to have caused my embarrassment. And, like a scolded child, I asked the Divine to look mercifully upon me because I truly felt the folks, whom I called enemies, were unkind and hash toward me during my unfortunate predicament. In forgiving, we open the door to healing our hurt and pain. We concede that we are similar, and most importantly, we accept that it is difficult for folks to meet prescribed standards successfully. When trouble comes, surrender to the divine Spirit within as quickly as you can, for it is in your surrender that you can take ownership of a bothersome situation and be able to cast off your burden and move on. When I get to a place where life forces me to give up control about an outcome, I am inclined to tie an imaginary knot, hang on, and wait for directions from within. Whatever the situation, our communication with the Divine through prayers will keep us grounded, and we will be alerted to proceed when the time is right. You see, God puts meaning into events that happen in our life; it is for us to take notice and participate. During scary moments, some people rely on other people's promises to come through for them. I say stand on the promises you make to your Self, trust your commitment to Self. Your obligations to Self will sustain you, and your Built-in Prayer Mechanism will provide you with the right words as you communicate with Spirit within. Tangible ways of handling matters will be revealed to make your journey stress-free. In your most challenging moments, be still—be still and know, trust in your commitment to Self. Remember, own your circumstances as they happen, give way, surrender quickly, let go, and let God in as you cast off the burden on the divine Spirit within; the divine Spirit will show you how to address your responsibility.

Fear of fear itself

Living makes us fearful in situations over which we have no control—the fear of world wars, devastating earthquakes, hurricanes, floods, thunderstorms, and a prophetic doomsday are fears that make folks tremble. Some of these occurrences are humbling and make for great learning. When your life seems topsy-turvy, and you're beset with fears of every kind, the only fear that counts is the fear of God. The Scriptures say: *Fear God and keep his commandments: for this is the whole duty of man* (Ecclesiastes 12:13).

If my spouse did not return home at a reasonable time, or if my daughter stayed out later than usual, or if a lab test was not to my liking, one or more of my fears would overpower me. Fear makes me crazy until I know the meaning of what may be happening at that moment. I learned first to acknowledge the things I am afraid of, summon all my strength, stand my ground, and address the things I fear. If your stomach turns and your mouth goes dry if your ears get hot and your pulse races out of control, then know that fear is trying to demolish you. Defeat fear when it confronts you by refusing to believe the lies fear tell. Know that most of the things you fear will likely not happen; the lies fear tells will confuse your mind and make you believe untruths. It is wise to fear an oncoming vehicle when crossing; however, we should not allow the fear of a motor vehicle accident to prevent us from driving our car.

When my fears cornered me, I created ingenious ways of doing and saying things to cover them up. I allowed my fears to control me to the extent that my fears dictated when and how I came and went and what I said and did. I showed a façade, but I fear, and I was fearful for other people, to be truthful. I was not consciously aware of how frequently I had been validating my fears. Be warned; your heart will attack you; obesity and hypertension will floor you, and cancers will find a way to inhabit your body and stay indefinitely if you continually give way to an occurring fear. I tell folks to recognize fear when it presents itself, pinpoints the mask it wears, then deals with it in a friendly way. Fear will shy away because fear is Ego in a different mask. Don't let fear drive you nuts. The song says: What have I to dread, what have I to fear, leaning on the everlasting arms?

—*Elisha A Hoffman/Anthony J Showalter*

Other people's fear

I have said that everything that is not our concern is other people's business, and time spent on other people's business cuts into the time we could spend tending to our own business. Other people's business includes other people's fears. Other people's fears will weave in and out of our life without our permission in subtle ways that will leave us fretful. For example, if we're financing someone's addictive habit, or trying to rescue someone from his or her chronic fears, or giving advice to someone who will never put into practice what we advise, we should know that we are meddling, not helping. Everyone should be cautious about uninvited involvements in other people's fears and habits. I call other people's fears and habits of other people's business. It is okay to be sympathetic and even feel other people's pain, but keep in mind we have enough of our fears to last us a lifetime. Address your fears. Fear is not just to be nervous or worried about a situation; fear is a condition that can spread. Fear is infectious. I learned this in a most unusual way when a friend of mine had to complete a particular medical test. She expressed to me her anxieties and asked me to explain to her how the procedure works. I never experienced a medical issue of that kind; therefore, I never had to do such a procedure. In the meantime, my friend's fear of the test and what the results might mean seeped into my psyche, so I asked my physician to arrange the same test for me. I got tested, and as a result, I was able to talk about the procedure with my friend, thereby helping to alleviate her fear.

Fear of judgments and criticisms

The folks who judge are those who assess someone, something, or a circumstance in a critical way. They are the people whose hair is not perfect, and they continuously need to lose ten pounds. Many people do not see themselves as enough, and they probably will never be satisfied with their appearance. It is hard not to measure against those around us who we see as successful; it is harder still not to measure against the person we used to be if we like that person better. Such comparisons only keep us stuck at a place where we'd rather not be. How then should we handle true Self when other people judge us? One option is to see other people's judgments as constructive criticisms. Rather than dwelling on how other people judge us, we should take what we can from objection and trust in Self to adjust our state of affairs. People tend to forget that they're wonderfully made; there is no need to alter or change anything—everything is as it should be. Consider a situation where you're judged in a most unflattering manner, and you try to defend yourself without success—what do you do? Free yourself from the conditions under which you were judged. By freeing yourself and taking action only when you're ready to bless, you're refusing to participate in the judgment cycle of blame and shame. Type A sisters and brothers genuinely believe they are right, and the other people are wrong. They think it is their responsibility to point out other people's faults and mete out appropriate verdicts.

Banish rages and panic attacks

I rolled out of bed late that morning thinking: *Thank God it's Friday.* I switched on the table lamp close by—no electricity. I rummaged through the mail on my kitchen counter, and there it was—the notice of disconnection. A silent prayer would have been appropriate at that moment. Instead, I freaked because I knew I was about to do battle with an assortment of fears. While I was on the telephone with the electricity company, negotiating re-connection, my doorbell rang. I opened my front door to see my girl-friend Celia from out of town standing on my steps—her hands waving wildly in the air. "Surprise," she exclaimed. My hair was uncombed, I had not yet brushed my teeth, I was grouchy, and there was no electricity in my house. "Surprise?"

I asked in a less than welcoming tone. Celia was taken aback by my response to her—a typical response should have been an invitation to come in. But fear of every kind took over my senses—fear of being exposed, fear of poverty, fear of loss of credibility, fear of loss of love—name any fear because I felt that fear at the moment. Fear will make us forget that we know what to do when sticky situations arise. Panic attacks and angry come-backs are kinds of fear showing up in another disguise. Did I think that I could continue to hide my fear of being irresponsible by ignoring my disconnection notice? Yes. Know that fear will lull us into thinking that all is well. We should address our fears when they confront us and not let them ripple and cause further problems. My electricity was reconnected that same day, and all was normal again. The anxiety I experienced that morning was a combination of my fears needing to be addressed. Under no circumstances should anyone say they'd rather not know about what's going on, be ready to deal with fearful issues. Know that fear is nothing; fear creates lies, tame fear with love when it raises its ugly head, and watch fear recoils into nothingness where it belongs.

The only fear that counts

Let's consider the only fear that matters—the fear of God. Fear of God includes faith, hope, and love. Fear of God is your belief in the divine Spirit within. The Scriptures say: The fear of the Lord is clean, enduring forever (Psalms 19:9). There is no need to gloss over fear with pretenses; face fear because fear is another tool from life's toolbox to be used as needed. Understand that fear comes, and fear goes, and some fears stay much longer than we may like, but when fear raises its ugly head, I suggest that you acknowledge that you are fearful, then change your thoughts about the specific fear—put a positive spin on fear. As you begin to think positively about your situations, fear will cower and fade away—no need to tolerate a perpetual state of anxiety or nervousness. The fact that fear puts folks on the same mental footing makes fear an equal companion; yes, I said companion because I truly believe fear is Ego wearing a different mask. Weaken the lies Ego promotes through the many faces of fear. Do not allow any of the manifestations of fear to cause you to throw your plans away or change plans that are dear to you. Revise the original plan; take a different route; wait for another moment; get a further diagnosis; ask for another opinion; change your outlook, and the lies fear promotes will dissolve. Fear of God lets us "standstill, and see." (*Exodus 14:13*). Remember this: the only fear that counts is the fear of God. Do not allow any of the manifestations of fear to cause you to throw your plans away or alter and make changes to plans which are dear to you; most of the things you fear will likely not happen; fear is nothing.

Between a rock and a hard place

When things aren't going well or when significant decisions are required, folks sometimes say they're between a rock and a hard place, and they genuinely believe the position they find themselves at that moment *is* a hard place. At that place, folks usually cannot remember how they got there or their role en route. And since they're already there, they would rather stay and play the victim game. The joke about the woman who fell into a deep hole comes to mind. The woman fell into a deep hole and could not climb out. Her physician walked by and handed her a drug prescription, which did not help her condition. Her priest later walked by and gave her a verse, and though she repeated the mantra umpteen times, her situation remained the same. Her best friend walked up and promptly slid down into the hole. The woman in the deep hole expressed shock that her best friend would do such a silly thing—now they both were in the deep hole. Her best friend said, "No worries, my friend, I have been in a deep hole like this before, we'll get out together." It is doubtful that folks will find themselves in uncomfortable places by accident.

Whether the place is hard or soft, the truth is folks participated in whatever took them to wherever they found themselves, and the sooner folks admit that fact, the sooner they will be strong enough to ask for and receive help. I cannot count the number of times I prayed with tears running down my cheeks, my duvet snotty and soiled from mascara, and my situation seemed to remain the same. Seemed is the operative word because looking back; I can say the answers to my prayers were clear—I just did not like the answers I received. Here are some things to remember: Begin your prayers by forgiving yourself for being unreasonable to you. Don't fall back on dramatics or resort to human rescues. Don't go telling your sad stories to everyone who will listen. Other people have their own tragic stories. It was difficult for me not to cry every time I heard Thelma as she told her sad story—with variations here and there.

The story goes like this: Thelma's boyfriend of five years broke up with her (by all accounts, for no good reason), she was evicted from her apartment because of unpaid rent, and she found herself in a situation where she had to decide between purchasing food for her three children and purchasing her diabetic medications. Did I mention that Thelma's case brought tears to my eyes? Always. It is unfortunate, but some folks are slow to recognize their deteriorating state-of-affairs. Recognizing *what is* would have alleviated the drama of the kind that Thelma experienced. I agree that Thelma's state of affairs was challenging. However, her situation did improve when she accepted counseling, which led her to seek diabetic medications through the local clinic. Thelma was then able to focus on taking proper care of her children—there is a way forward without shame, blame, and drama.

Acknowledge what is going on

It is untrue to say that life's journey will always be smooth and free from challenges, although some folks would like other folks to believe that all is well with them all the time. Those are the folks who forget that they live in a world with the *other* folks. They will say: *they're in the world but not of the world.* I say be honest about how your life is unfolding and be ready to change with it, embrace life in every way. Know that life consists of night and day, back and front, inside and outside, ups and downs, good and not so good.

The fear game we call blame

Quite often, we play the fear game to cover up or shift responsibility to someone else. On the one hand, blame may help when folks find themselves in tight spots; on the other hand, guilt can cause chaos and confusion. If we have to blame our mother, our father, our sister, our brother, our spouse, and the dog, we know we have not paid attention to our Self. I am not saying that people should not be made to take responsibility for their destructive behaviors and foolish decisions; however, blaming others is never the best course of action. Accepting or dishing out blame is a tactic of fear to cover up irresponsible behavior. I say address a sticky situation neutrally and avoid being caught up in casting blame or accepting fault. Understand that everyone is innocently making his or her way through life. People and conditions change moment-by-moment. Blame no one and take no blame.

Some people learn the same lessons repeatedly

Some people are slow learners; they are slack about directions, and as a result, they may be required to take extra lessons to keep up with the class. Other people think they already have the answers and they have no need to hit the books. Touché. Learning indicates growth—I say, learn, and grow. If folks are blasé about learning, they will probably be stuck at the back of the classroom of life. However, if folks are serious, they will benefit from lessons that will advance them to the front of the class. Some folks learn the same lessons repeatedly, perhaps under different circumstances, so that they may thoroughly absorb the course. And life will put folks in classes for advanced learning to teach them vital lessons. Incarcerated individuals might be demonstrating to other life travelers a path that should be avoided. People who practice spirituality know that their thoughts are manifested moment-by-moment. They know that unless they express their views honestly and own the experiences that come from their thoughts, they will find it hard to move ahead in life's classroom. In the school of life, a lesson does not go away until it is fully learned. Incidents occur for learning and should be seen as valuable. Life will insist we learn and relearn a lesson until we get it. Learn and grow.

Say no to whatever you don't want

It is not unusual for some folks to find themselves in a classroom for failed relationships—they're there to learn valuable life lessons about the love they want and need and the love they truly deserve. Folks hang on to relationships that have long been over or form new relationships that look and feel like the failed ones. Life will give folks more of what they seek until they are sure about what they truly desire. Don't linger in failed relationships longer than necessary, even though you know it to be far better to learn the lesson as it is presented and make the next a better one. Annie regularly complains that her relationships are often verbally abusive, no matter that the relationships began civilly and courteously. On one occasion, I asked Annie why she thought she was attracting abuse. She replied that the words *disrespect me* must be written across her forehead. I told her that if such words were written across her forehead, she was the one who wrote and put them there. Annie did not take too kindly to my statement. People should say no to what they don't want or be offered the same things repeatedly. Unattractive words come from negative thoughts; negative thoughts should be changed. Own your emotions and release the ones you don't want.; loving thoughts, lonesome feelings, hateful retorts, jealous rages, angry responses, own all of them. If they come from you, they are your manifestations. Some emotions may make you bawl when you consider your foolishness, or you may laugh at a feeling you feel to be amazingly funny. Remember this: life will give you what you seek; be sure about what you truly desire.

Don't be quick to show indifference

People will show indifference even in circumstances where they're judged incorrectly, slandered viciously, called names they dare only whisper, or blatantly taken advantage of—they will act as though they were not offended. Know that you may be unintentionally pulling more negative responses toward you when you show indifference in those circumstances. I say, examine situations that bring disrespect—find out why such things are happening. Dorothy had seen the signs long before she confirmed Eric's infidelity—it was not just his open disrespect for her, his absence from the dinner table, and his tardiness with the household bills—it was also his glaring lack of appetite for her affections. She had started to blame herself for Eric's non-response when she happened upon his infidelity. Dorothy hunkered down in guilt and became indifferent in her stance towards Eric. Her attitude encouraged Eric to continue his irresponsible behavior. An emotion of indifference is a disguise used by Ego to discourage Self and a reason to ignore the occurring circumstances with an *I don't care*; attitude—meaning if folks don't care, then the situation won't matter. Some people use indifference to point out things they are willing to *take* or *leave* in a given moment.

Every reason to show indifference is a cover-up, and sooner or later, life will force the folks who cover up to show up. How do you cover up your indifference? Do you cover up as a workaholic? Do you cover up as an alcoholic? Do you use religious affiliations as a disguise? Is your disrespectful manner your cover-up? Do you just turn a blind eye and ignore what is going on? Individuals who respond to sticky situations with a show of indifference could lose the respect of others. It is appropriate to inquire why your spouse, your children, friends, and neighbors show disregard in the face of challenges. I used to express my indifference by saying, to hell with the consequences, and then I proceeded with my plan. That was not a good reaction because the realities presented to me later were not always ones I appreciated. Some folks might express their indifference by saying: *That will never happen to me,* and then carry on regardless. Don't be quick to show indifference. An emotion of boredom in any situation diminishes your influence and may be seen by other folks as laughable or perhaps pathetic. How do you cover-up? Jordan was always late for work, his projects were regularly incomplete, and he skipped important meetings. Jordan complained that his boss was unfriendly to him for no reason. The fact is, Jordan's boss elected to cover up his annoyance with Jordan by being cold and indifferent.

Have a point of view

My point of view is the one certainty I will not compromise; my statements and positions are steadfast. My point of view is the boldness with which I put forward my ideas; it is how I make my approach; it is my expression. I believe that my point of view is a true companion to my opinion. What is your point of view? Is your point of view *your* honest opinion? Is your point of view contingent on another person's beliefs? People who don't bother to put forward a point of view should know that life will assign a point of view that may not suit their purpose. Many of us know or are acquainted with people who do not want to get involved in situations that are not of concern. They have nothing to say and do not care to give an opinion. Such individuals will sit on the sidelines without a point of view until life makes a decision for them—a decision, I might add, that may or may not be to their liking, or they may attach themselves to the point of view that looks good at that moment. I spent an enormous amount of time listening to other peoples' viewpoints and opinions; I absorbed their negative and unworthy criticisms. I allowed others to exercise their power and influence over me. Very often, I swayed back and forth like a trunk-less sapling—always second-guessing my decisions. When you know and state your point of view, no one can successfully *pull the wool* over your eyes or influence your choices. Other people's opinions that previously kept you mired in negative situations become pointless and undeserving of your attention.

When I was diagnosed as hypertensive, I was agreeable to the point of saying the diagnosis was not surprising because hypertension runs in my family's genes. As a matter of course, I accepted the diagnosis and remained on medication for many years until my point of view regarding hypertension changed. A point of view, such as the one I had about a severe diagnosis as hypertension, was uninformed. Armed with a different perspective and a new attitude, I discussed with my physician other ways to take care of my condition and decided on one that suited the management of my hypertension with less medication, more exercise, and a wholesome diet. Express your point of view! Your clearly expressed point of view will manifest a feeling that is worthy of consideration. Your point of view might be the opinion or the remark that could sway an outcome or positively alter a critical decision. When you state your point of view, no one can successfully *pull the wool* over your eyes.

And make your point of view real!

Let's consider a woman I am acquainted with who endured an abusive spousal union longer than was necessary. I have to say; I admired her courage because she escaped the situation with her three small children and found shelter in a religious home for abused wives, a family that seemed safe and peaceful and one that she thought was the answer to her prayers. But she encountered a situation of abuse and control in new and different ways. Before long, she discovered that the religious setting was definitely not the alternative she desired, and she sought dwelling elsewhere. Whether your world is an abusive family home or a controlling church community, if you do not have a point of view, you will likely not have an opinion and maybe slow in making the right decisions on your behalf. It is spiritually healthy to make alternative decisions.

Know that one unhappy relationship will ripple into more unhappy relationships, for when folks are not clear about what *you* desire or what *you* are willing to accept, folks will give more of what they think you want. You can be sure that others will put forward one for you if you don't have a point of view.

Have a point of view, be ready to express your point of view, and where appropriate, defend your point of view. Your point of view might be your defense in a sticky situation.

Surrender is a spiritual act of faith

Jocelyn worked as a personal support worker in a home care establishment for twenty-five years. Jocelyn was stunned when her employer handed her a notice of lay off. PSW is what Jocelyn knows and does best, but she feared her age might be a factor in finding a similar job. I suggested to Jocelyn that she brings together two or three of her colleagues who were also laid off from the same establishment to discuss the idea of starting a similar business. Jocelyn squirmed at the idea, but she took my advice. Jocelyn now owns a small but successful home care business. Out of fear, some folks will contrive countless reasons not to surrender a state-of-affairs or act in faith as Spirit directs. Folks should know that spiritual relief comes in many ways—verbally through discussions, suggestions, and advice; and most definitely through feelings. When I was called to publish my prayers, I figured the idea would be okay. I reasoned that I could pick and choose the prayers I wanted to print because my prayers were of significance to only me. One day, while I was sweating my prayers underneath my duvet (comforter), I was pressed to share all of my written prayers—my negative thoughts, my fears, my resentments, my anger, and everything that was *ugly* and ungodly about me—announce them to everyone! I recognized that the call to expose my emotional prayers was a significant life assignment. So I was hesitant to bare my negativities (which I thought might be seen as selfish, jealous, spiteful, fearful, angry, and down-right unattractive by other folks). But I published the pleasant and the not so attractive traits about me and I encouraged folks to express their own true feelings as I did, in the hope that they may become familiar with their true Self.

Heavenly Father
My prayers were written to You, for my relief and for my eyes only. I am not qualified or even worthy to express in writing because everything I write may be judged as right or wrong
Direct my thoughts so that my writings will be for Your honor and Your glory and in Your name.
(Olive Rose Steele)

Like me, you may not want to announce your call to surrender; your surrender is your reliance on God's faithfulness to you. Know that God listens to every prayer of surrender from all of his children. He will direct and guide you to completion. Always remember, when you surrender, you give up the desire to be a victim of your circumstances; you decide to release all outcomes, and you tell your Ego there is no more room in your heart to play dollhouse.

Say yes to the call to surrender

My Surrender was my call to admit that I possess nothing. Divine Spirit uses every one of us, moment-by-moment to deliver spiritual relief to others; divine Spirit operates on its terms for the good of everyone. You may be a dressmaker or a hairdresser, but when life calls you to surrender, you may realize that you are indeed an inspiration to others. You may be an actor or a dancer, but when life calls you to surrender, you may recognize you are a healer of broken hearts. You may be an educator, but when life calls you to surrender, you may realize you are much more than a life coach. And like me, you are a fellow life traveler, and life may be calling you at this moment to surrender to a particular assignment. Answer the call; surrender. For Pam, surrender meant she had to give up custody of her children to her ex-husband. Pam found it challenging to quit substance abuse, and as a consequence, Pam lost custody of her children to her husband, Frank. The point is, folks who don't recognize when they arrive at a surrender point will inadvertently yield to other folks to make surrender decisions for them, and those decisions might not be the ones desired. Remember this: surrender is a spiritual act of faith; when you surrender you give up the need to be a victim of your circumstances. Spiritual relief comes when you surrender.

Surrender all

What does it mean to surrender all? All of what? In the past, I've said yes and surrendered. No, not really. I've said yes and surrendered selective things. Not everything. I held on to remnants, scraps, bits and pieces of things that call attention to my Ego. I held on to my excessive spending lifestyle until it gave me up—credit and loans *dried up*. Some people don't trust the divine Spirit to lead and direct matters. Me? I have to run things myself to be sure things will work to my advantage, and I have been wrong every time I *ran things*. When I tried to make sure things work to my satisfaction, I messed things up, and sometimes I messed up other people's things. As an act of surrender, I cast everything that holds me back on the divine Spirit within and go free—not because I am irresponsible but, as a child of God, because it is the right thing to do. Hanging in there when the signs indicate it is time to surrender might not be such a good thing. I say, let it go and let God in.

People and things will give up on us

People we love and admire might exit our life for no apparent reason; hell might "break loose," causing someone to decide to end a relationship, or we might damage and destroy valuable things. Individuals and things come into our life for a reason and definitely for a season; therefore, things that no longer have relevancy will disappear when the purpose is served and the season ends. Indeed, we may not want to give up certain things; I say "bite the bullet" and give them up. Lay down everything you think you *must* keep, but you know you *should* give up, lighten your load—give them up—see how much more comfortable you will breathe. Do not struggle to understand the meanings and the whys and wherefores of what may be happening in your moment. Love Self, even when others abandon you—when you show love for Self, you can survive when things and people give you up. Do trust the divine Spirit to lead and direct matters, know that stuff with no relevancy will disappear with time, recognize when you arrive at a surrender point, know that when things and people served the purpose, the season ends.

Things are usually not how they appear

"Judge not, that he be not judged. For with what judgment ye judge, ye shall be judged: and with what measure ye mite, it shall be measured to you again." (*Matthew 7:1-2*) I am one among many who judge out of fear, anger, resentment, and negativity, and I find that other people's fears always put me in mutual meddling. Every time we look critically or act unforgivingly, we are judgmental. Judgments indeed allow us to adjust or change, and because we are not perfect, we should always welcome feedback from others—positive or otherwise.

Since judgments are our own opinions, views, thoughts, and feelings, then one person's judgment should not be considered sounder than the next person's judgment. And whether an assessment is viewed as a judgment or feedback, the individual doing so would be wise to be cautious. Those who give feedback should know that the line between feedback and judgment is thin—what may be happening at the moment may not be the whole picture. Things are usually not how they seem, and that is why folks ought to think through what they're called upon to judge. By reflecting on the outcome, folks can release other folks from burdensome guilt. Consider the ten-year-old girl familiar with the tale; *Little Red Riding Hood,* she is anxious to perform, but her tutor assesses her as too tall to play the role of *Little Red Riding Hood.* Or the skilled employee is passed over for promotion in the Firm because she *falls short* of the required years-of-service.

How folks are judged is not always accurate; know that you are not how other folks may assess you—you are what you can be; that is why folks should be flexible when making judgments.

Remember, we are not called to judge; we should love. We should speak to goodness that characterizes all of us. Let's recognize everyone, including those we identify as enemies or rivals, as people seeking fairness.

Is something wrong?

Circumstances are neutral and don't always synchronize. That's just the way life is. It is not fair to blame yourself, and it is worse when you accept blame from someone. The phrase "Is something wrong?" is often followed by the word *with*. People believe something is usually wrong *with* someone or something. Nothing is wrong with you and me. Wait—I will clarify. Consider this—we are kept alive by our beating heart and the lifesaving air that we breathe, and we can grow into our true potential—proof that we did not show up here by accident and evidence that nothing is wrong with us.

When the plans of folks who are not yet enlightened get *messed up*, they might assume that something was wrong, and they will declare that whatever was wrong could only have been their fault and must be mended by them. Things don't happen because something was right or wrong; things happen because every other *thing* is dependent on something else—the one has to harmonize with the other for the whole to come together in perfect ways. When things did not turn out the way you intended or expected, rethink the decision, believe it was most likely not the right time to manifest the desired result. Step back, assess the situation as an uninvolved bystander, and acknowledge that it is happening without blame or fault.

Keeping pace without my GPS and Blackberry often makes me question whether my day will turn out good or not so good, and many times I marvel at how I functioned in the past without these devices. Much of the pain and discomfort in our life happens when we try to make things right. Right and wrong are responsibilities we *dish* out. Folks should recognize that their right might not be right for others. Wrong allows someone else to say they are right. Wrong calls you a liar. Wrong keeps folks in unhealthy places and retards their progress. Wrong concedes that someone else should call the shots. Right and wrong come from a mindset of perfection—remember, circumstances are neutral and don't always synchronize; everything just *is*. I am suggesting that individuals accept life as a process of continuous learning. I believe the reason life unfolds moment by moment is to keep humans equal. Yes, folks can draw from examples of previous moments to determine the next moment, but I believe that when folks look closely in prior moments, they will notice differences, which will confirm the view that no one knows what the next moment will look like. The next time you're of a mind to ask, "Is something wrong?" I suggest you say instead, "I love it when a plan comes together." See things as neutral.

Dear God
This situation makes me feel helpless
I release my opinions; I relinquish my ideas
I lay down my human will
I put aside my human planning
I give up my human ambitions
I abandon my human pride and vanity
I now give this heavy burden to You, Father
Govern this situation; take full control of the outcome
And bless everyone involved.
(*And When We Pray*)

Possessions and "things" or lesser gods

People own essential things, sentimental things, luxurious things, and expensive things. All of us—you and I have personal effects that serve us. Our possessions and things provide for our healthy, happy, and wholesome living. Our possessions and things tell other folks that we are successful. I often tell people to protect and appreciate their possessions and things. But, when we experience upheavals and disruptions that we do not understand, approve of, or want, and when our possessions and things begin to break, fear of every kind will overtake us. We fear that the folks who are acquainted with us may find out that we no longer have our valuables, and we may lose their admiration. I call possessions *things*—not to devalue or trivialize but to be reminded that possessions and things tend to appear and disappear. While it is reasonable to appreciate and protect our things, we should try not to overvalue them. All of us—you and I—have possessions and things we adore; these things might be called lesser gods.

Wait, I will explain. If you think you cannot live without certain possessions and hold these possessions in high regard, these possessions are your lesser gods. Today's living makes it easy for some folks to be loyal to their possessions and things, and if folks are not vigilant, these things can quickly turn into lesser gods. Lesser gods will abandon us. They will break, crumble into little pieces, be stolen or lost, and may simply disappear for no apparent reason. We should seriously consider the role lesser gods play in our lives and not allow lesser gods to blur our vision. If loyalty to possessions and things blurs our vision, it is time to call possessions and things what they truly are: *lesser gods*.

We are proof of divine approval, we are custodians of *Her* blessings, and we are charged to make sure *Her* gifts to us are not turned into lesser gods. Lesser gods are never faithful to us. Julia appreciated her possessions and things. She protected them as best she could, then one day, she lost everything she owned in a terrible rainstorm. It is challenging to encourage levelheadedness in situations like the kind Julia experienced. To suggest that Julia trust God, the Divine Provider might not be pragmatic advice to unbelievers like her. In the end, Julia received donations to replace most of the things she lost in the storm.

Why do folks hang on to "things"?

My daughter once asked me, "Mommy, why do you hang on to things?" She was referring to my refusal to accept what *is*. I wanted to tell my daughter the things I hang on to make me happy. There were times when I had to be knocked down and dragged across the floor before I came to my senses and let go of things that were millstones. Folks should know that with divine guidance, most of the things they hang on to can just as quickly be given up. Are some of your things your lesser gods? Why are you not willing to de-clutter? Is fear the issue? Is letting go and letting God in hard to do? If you answered *yes* to any of these questions, then take heart you are not alone. It is not unusual for folks to want to keep their things, especially those things that serve them well. I am suggesting, right now, at this moment, letting go of everything you think you *must* keep. Place all the things which make you tremble at the thought of losing on your altar of sacrifice, inhale several deep breaths—breathe out. You will marvel at how easily you breathe after you've let things go. That something or someone served the purpose intended, and it was time to let go.

Recognizing a toxic situation and accepting that it is time to let go and move on is hard, but know that you have performed a spiritual act of courage when you yield. Things fall apart, get lost, break and expire, not necessarily frustrate or punish, but alert you to an important life lesson.

Dear God,
I am sitting in a lonely valley
Hemmed beneath a high mountain
This place is strange and uncomfortable
I cannot remember when or even how I got here
Shine a light in this cold and isolated place
Help me find my way out, Give me the strength to endure as I claw my way to safety
I now cast this burden on the Christ within
And wait for my miracle, In Jesus Name.
(And When We Pray)

Your possessions and things show the desires of your heart. Appreciate your possessions and things; they are your hard work on display. Protect your possessions and things; they are your answered prayers. Love your possessions and things; they are your blessings. Enjoy your possessions and things while they serve you. Trust that you already have all the possessions and things you need to survive this life. Recognize when your possessions and things are turning into *lesser gods* and apply spiritual discernment as a way of keeping your Self evenly balanced. Many of the things you hang on to can be given up to free you from unnecessary burdens.

You don't have to hang in there

Some people let go and let God into their life after praying the quick *Help me, Lord*, with one eye open. Others let go after they have been knocked down on both knees with both eyes shut—begging, pleading, imploring with streams of tears rolling down their cheeks. Folks should know that it is not their duty to decide ahead of the answers to their prayers. The Scriptures tell us: "He shall receive the blessing from the Lord, and righteousness from the God of his Salvation." (*Psalms 24:5-7*) Our prayer requests are delivered in amazing ways by Helpers sent by our Heavenly Father, Giver of good gifts. People are busy taking care of their moment-by-moment survival; they forget that they are sheltered and protected by an invisible hand that is continuously at work in their lives. I have learned to quickly take responsibility for my fears to hand over my circumstances to the One who has the solutions. Have faith—know that things that frighten you are things you can usually handle. If it feels like you are swimming against the tide or the tide is coming too fast, you should know it is time to yield and wait for smoother waves to come in. A rising tide indicates that life is not flowing as you like it—surrender.

When we stumble, God indicates a change in strategy—a signal to take a different path. Accept that the method you are engaging in might not be the right one. I did wake up because it was time to cast the burden of a Company that aggravated my stomach ulcers on the divine Spirit within and go free. I did change course, even though my ambition encouraged me to stay on the same track. I admit I was angry at myself for all the things that went wrong. Yet, I withdrew my emotional attachments long enough to accept that the things I experienced in those moments, as awful as I thought they were, had been my thoughts, words, and feelings showing up in undesirable ways.

Change is good

"Follow your bliss, the rest is just smoke and mirrors." — Jessica Fletcher (as Angela Lansbury) in TV series: *Murder, She Wrote*

My husband drove his minivan until it turned into an old clunker. After many tries, I succeeded in convincing him to turn it in for a more efficient vehicle. He walked into the car dealership holding a business card from the salesman who completed the deal some years earlier. He was sympathetic to learning about the passing of his former salesman. However, he was visibly upset that he would have to trust a different salesperson to advise him on his new purchase. My husband believes things should stay the same—always. Change for many people might not be as simple as purchasing a new motor vehicle or dealing with a new salesperson—change may very well be a significant shift that turns life in a completely new and different direction. Eric's extra-marital affair was a devastating discovery for his wife Dorothy. Eric wanted to remain married to protect his image as a family man, but Dorothy would not stand for Eric's infidelity; she divorced Eric even though she knew that a break-up would be a major change for her. Marriage break-ups, relationship issues, financial upheavals, emotional stress, and health challenges are frightening situations that could change people's lives in remarkable ways. Such problems might plunge folks into a personal *valley* for a very long time. Notwithstanding the loneliness folks might experience in *valley* situations, folks may emerge in *one piece* because of faith in their ability to persevere.

It may not be easy to change the job that adequately sustains our family. It could be challenging to change from an unhappy, toxic relationship that shelters our children to a situation of uncertainty. It is tough to change a lifestyle we've always controlled to one of total surrender. We will put off, procrastinate, wait a little longer, hope for a better day and time, if you will because many of us are slow to change. Be warned, when Spirit signals a change, obey. Recognize that a change might just be the antidote for what may be wrong in your moment; try a new thing. Like me, you may try to resist the changes you thought could shatter the foundation of your life—those are changes we call unfair. Letting go of what we can see, feel, and touch requires us to trust that all will be well in the end. In accepting what is, we are trusting that through faith, we possess the tools necessary to make the right decisions; we are trusting that the decisions we make will be suitable for that moment. This was real in my life when I surrendered an admired business address and relocated to a less expensive address. Life will back us into a corner and force us to make significant changes or agree to major decisions so that we may put our situations in order. Change is good; a shift in attitude might be the cure for your illness; this might be the moment to consider a change of address, change your thinking, change your life, a shift in strategy signals fresh ideas, and have faith in your ability to persevere.

When is the right time for a change?

George's foolish ways of handling his finances caught up with him when his girlfriend discontinued his free boarding and asked him to vacate the apartment they had been sharing. George turned to his cousin Janice for temporary shelter. The fifth month came, and George was still sleeping on Janice's couch; Janice pointedly told George to *hit the road* at the end of the fifth month—right move, right time. Mary is the employee at her desk every morning before the others come to work, and she is the employee everyone tells *goodnight* when they leave the office at the end of the day. Mary's position with the company makes her eligible for promotions, which she never got. Mary was courageous; she gave up the job and started her own business—the right move. When you're paying attention to what's going on around you, you will know the right time to take action. The issue is not that folks don't know when it is the right time for action; the problem is that folks are unwilling to make the change. The right time is when you say and do things as Spirit leads; the right time is when you uproot yourself from everything you're grounded in and step into an unfamiliar space, in faith. Your right time might not be suitable for other people—make your change anyway. Your right time might be now.

Use change to your advantage

People have a hunch about their possibilities. They may be pursuing a specific profession, yet in the background of their consciousness is the idea that they would rather be doing something different. Something different is what they would love to do but are afraid to tackle because other people may not approve. Call it your potential, bliss, dream, happiness, and true love; above all, call it change.

 The day came when I felt I should be pursuing something different. My simmering imagination presented itself in a most unusual way—deep down, tucked away in my consciousness, was my desire to write. As I wrote down my views and expressed my feelings, I was amazed at how easily my words flowed and formed sentences that turned into numerous pages. Don't delay; make your change.

And make major shifts

Once-a-year I clear out old clothes and shoes from my closet, I discard empty boxes and shopping bags, shred old letters, greeting cards, and expired papers, and recycle everything recyclable. At the end of the exercise, I see a clearer picture, and invariably I find essential things I had been searching for. I use the same comparison about my state of mind to clear out the clutter that piles up in my mind's closet. I was ready to make significant shifts. I had no idea where to begin, but I collected boxes and mentally packed them in my mind. I couldn't carry everything, and, in any event, some things were junk and needed to be ditched. The thought that my husband could not survive without my unsolicited advice was ill-fitting and needed to perish. I had to believe that my granddaughters would love me anyway, even though my main concern was no longer their beck and call. Like me, you may still be hanging on to your mother's and perhaps your grandmother's colds and fever remedies—believe me, the pharmacy brands work faster. The ancient Dutch oven that my grandmother swore bubbles up its own flavors was turned over to my husband to get the flavors going. I put my faith in divine Spirit to remove the cobwebs and dust that clouded my thoughts; those out-of-style ideas about right and wrong began to disappear. I cast off outdated ideas that held me in a straitjacket for a significant part of my life. Views and opinions were thrown out to make space for fresh new ideas; my mind was no longer weighty. Conversations with my girl- and guy-friends that once had my attention no longer received my full hearing. My mental wardrobe looked differently. New thoughts and ideas made sense. *I bundled-up* the old ideas I used to call sentimental, put them on a heap, and placed a sign atop the pile that read "disposables," then I breathed a sigh of relief.

The familiar old style that characterized who I had been changed. I acknowledged my authentic Self and reasoned there was no need to apologize for being me. I answered *yes* or *no* and truly meant it. Gather up all your disposables and dispose of them! My guy-friend Eric disclosed to me his unlucky "streak" with female relationships. I reminded Eric that he was recovering from his divorce, and he was probably missing his ex-wife Dorothy. Eric disagreed with my point of view and continued to moan about his bad luck with women. Eric's issues needed more than a *sounding board*; he needed an expert fixer of irrational thinking. Eric needed to see clearly.

Deacon Willie (may his soul rest in peace) had difficulty being honest about his junk disposal. A married, religious churchman, Deacon Willie convinced himself and his congregation that his spiritual closet was clear of all junk and cobweb. But in the corner of his spiritual closet was his pornography addiction. Deacon Willie's pornographic secret came to light most embarrassingly and shamefully before he passed. Put discipline into your life; discipline helps you to give up sinful practices—those practices are your *skeletons* in your closet, and your *skeletons* will come out to scare you; disciplined individuals spend more time praying, meditating, praising, and being honest with Self. Put order into your life; order points to where the litter and waste (junk) in our life is. Order gives a clear picture of your thoughts; order makes sure everything is in its proper place. If you want to bring new energy into your life, then you have to let go of bad habits—junk.

"I think I can make it now the pain is gone/All of the bad things have disappeared/Here's the rainbow I've been praying for/It's gonna be a bright (bright) sun-shiny day."
—*Johnny Nash*

If you are experiencing pain and the bad things won't disappear, then it is time to clear away the rubble. Clean out your junk closet; make way for right-fitting thoughts and actions—ease your pain. Do not ignore rotting waste; gather up your junk (bad habits), bundle them up, and throw them out with the garbage. If the exercise is too much work, I say, hire an expert fixer of junk habits to help you clear your mind.

Practice makes perfect

Every day, I repeat to myself, "I am happy, I am loving, I am healthy, and I am whole." That's because I believe *I am* happy, *I am* loving, *I am* healthy, and *I am* whole. When we practice, we're making sure that our practice's thing or subject stays at the forefront of our consciousness. Until now, some people were unaware that repetition and practice happen every moment in their life. People who are aware of their repeated practices make changes and grow, although every time folks go against old recurrences with new ways, the old repetitions challenge them right back. I have said that the things I broke and lost were significant, yet I repeated losing things. Why? I was not paying attention to my repeats. Recurrences will creep up when people aren't paying attention. People who rehearse and practice positively will find nothing in other folks to judge; they know that all are children of God searching for new ways to rehearse and practice.

Know that Faith in what you practice assures that everything rehearsed and practiced will be well-learned because practice makes perfect. What is your practice? Do you pay attention to the things you say and do? Do you realize that you repeat some things more frequently? Confidence in whatever you practice will allow you to repeat, knowing that everything will work out for your good; you can affirm with certainty the things you believe and practice. Focus on your practice, pay attention to your repeats; see how your life appears differently when you practice to speak softly, listen sensibly, and act graciously.

Accept!

When you accept, you're doing far more than *not* rejecting a person, a condition, and a thing; you embrace the situation, person, and a thing as truth; you are acting with certainty and confidence. My husband and I were negotiating the purchase of a new home—a critical decision because funds from the sale of another property were contingent on purchasing the new house. Our mortgage broker presented to us an agreement for our conditional purchase. Still, my husband and I were not certain that our other property's conditional sale would be reasonably completed; we rejected the purchase and the sale deal. It is sensible and practical for folks to be confident, if not guaranteed, about an outcome before they accept. *Accept* is an obligation to Self. Let's consider *accept* as an objection—non-acceptance if you will. Many people will not accept hunger, poverty, and ill-health as a fact of their life; they will not accept disrespect and dishonor as given; they will not accept a *look* that they disapproved of, and many will balk at family genes that are less than eye-catching. I put forward a spiritual mindset to non-acceptance—I say, everything is beautiful in its own way, and in God's eyes, everyone is perfect. Accept!

PART THREE:
OUR FAITHFUL DEEDS

Our faithful deeds are responsible things that we do within the limits of our circumstances regularly to show respect for life and the environment, without causing unnecessary stress on our resources and routine.

EVERYONE CAN TAKE stock of his faithful deeds. Take my husband, for example; some of his faithful acts are done in our home, like tightening up every dripping faucet, turning off every unnecessary light, and preparing our refuse for pick up and disposal once every week. My faithful deeds are different. I will drop my last dollar in the panhandlers' can, share the fees for a friend's parking ticket, and groom my 89-year-old girl-friend Rosie's hair. Your faithful deeds might be your regular blood donations and the effort you make to recycle your recyclables. Our faithful acts are responsible things that we do within the limits of our circumstances regularly to show respect for life and the environment, without causing unnecessary stress on our resources and routine.

Our faithful deeds, do they matter?

Taking part in devotional worship, baptisms, confirmations, and holy communions are faithful activities that help folks maintain their beliefs and strengthen their faith. Faithful deeds (actions) tend to matter much more to the folks who participate. My girl-friend Rosie never showed a strand of hair out of place because my faithful deed was to groom her hair. Our faithful acts should occur regularly and effortlessly with love and kindness. Develop faithful deeds, dedicate to them, and make someone happy.

Great is Thy Faithfulness

Show of love is a faithful Deed

"To generate true love, you need to know how it differs from attachment. Ordinary Love and compassion are intertwined with attachment because their motivations are selfish. You care about certain people because they temporarily help you or your friends."
—His Holiness the Dalai Lama, *How to Expand Love*

"Learning to love yourself and learning to love your brother go hand in hand. You can't love your brother and hate yourself, or love yourself and hate your brother."
—Paul Ferrini, *Love Without Conditions*

"Stop in the name of love/Think it over."
—Diana Ross and the Supremes

As an act, love is a faithful deed that makes one person accepts another person's kindness, meaning love will make folks say yes to tenderness and kindness. I describe love as having great affection for someone or something, a special fondness, and warm feelings for the object of one's desires. I used to believe a *touchy-feely* experience was the only practical affirmation of love. I thought love should cater to me, my desires, my wants, and my needs. I believed the term *True love* was coined to accommodate folks who wanted to hang on to other folks' affections. I made demands on other attachments and only cared about the people whom I believed cared about me. I loved *myself* only when everything was going my way. I loved *myself* more when other people expressed their love for me. I used to believe that only the love of other people mattered. For a long time, I thought that love should only return to itself. In the words of His Holiness, the Dalai Lama, my kind of love was "ordinary love."

How great is your love?

When I think about all the things humans share—the earth and its natural gifts, sun, moon, air, oceans, rivers, lakes, streams, kindred spirits, and so much more—things which keep us alive, just because God creates us, I exclaim—awesome! And when I think of how disorganized, messy, suspicious, fearful, resentful, vengeful, and quite often unloving I am, nonetheless, God loves me I say—Hallelujah! And because I am safe in the love of God, I can share my love with fellow life travelers. Acknowledge love as a faithful deed that makes people happy. Love gives (not take); love of Self draws others to express their love; the love of others might not be solely attached to you; accept love as given; recognize that love always returns to itself; give love and see the abundance of love that comes back to you.

Love takes care of every detail

Folks will come and go, in and out of our life for a reason and possibly for a season. Some folks will be faithful to us; others will not. Folks can choose to see other loves as conditional, or they can choose to see a love they can genuinely return. Don't sweat the measure and size of a love package or deliver love; just be with your love blessings. Each of us, in every moment, is being used by the Divine to complete *Her* love. When you know that love has taken care of every detail of your life, you experience complete freedom to be you. Love is never late, love is kind, love is patient, love is not boastful, and love is always looking out for your best interests even when it does not seem that way. I was going crazy. My husband pulled my strings earlier that morning.

I screamed at the mailman for misdirecting an essential piece of mail, and I forgot to bring home my favorite pair of shoes from the office. By the time I got to the grocery store, I was totally ticked. I was in no frame of mind to accept that the item I intended to return could not be processed without producing an original receipt. I was fit to be tied. I rummaged through my purse. No receipt. I had to go back home, and my husband would gloat. My husband smirked and watched me as I stormed off to the grocery store a second time, huffing and puffing. I was unloving to several people, including myself that particular morning.

Unloving acts come with feelings of guilt. Now, I show love to others in the way I wanted to be loved. Unless I was willing to give the love I sought, I should not expect to receive the love I deserve. People experience and touch love in all aspects of their lives, and often they express love in moments when they were not aware of their gestures. For example, the people who stay at home to look after the needs of their family show great love, individuals who dutifully show up in offices, in factories, behind counters, and around wheels—on time, every day, year in and year out—are practitioners of love. Your love is *missed* when you don't show up. Love is what we feel when we admit that we cannot be right if we make our sisters wrong; love is what we give even though our brothers hurt our feelings; love is how we display our beauty to the world. Love is the name we call our spouse. Love is the name we call our children. Love is our connection to the love of other folks. Love is the reason we forgive ourselves so that we can forgive others. Love is how we know there are no judgments. Enemy thoughts against the nature of love will remind us of the reasons love did not work out for us the last time; enemy thoughts will pop up to show us why we should not trust love this time; enemy thoughts will jog our memory about how cruel unreturned love can be. Give love.

Great is Thy Faithfulness

Until the 12th of never, I'll still be loving you

I have acted in unloving ways because I was insecure and doubtful about myself. Nevertheless, my husband continues to hold the mirror up to my face to show my unloving reflection. My unloving thinking lets me change how I replicate love. It is never about our brand of love or how we identify love; it's about God's love for us. Knowing that but for greater love than ours, we would not be alive at this point.

We maintain key relationships for a long time, and we often connect those relationships with love. We say nothing can or will separate us from such loves. But time is the greatest judge of how strong our love is—time will put our love to the test in ways that bring tears. Time will make us renew our love for our Self and others. Some people are not quick to form attachments; they are not prepared to give an ounce of love. Don't be stingy with your love. Don't question who delivers your love parcel. Don't sweat the measure and size of a love package. Love takes care of every detail of your life. Love is never late. Enjoy your love gifts. Do remember, Ego does not like it when folks extend love to others; Ego is at work in people's lives, moment to moment, making sure that folks guard their own love; Ego reminds folks to get value for the love they give; give love as a faithful deed.

Love the ones you're with

We are busy people. Our space is limited, and so we are fussy about whom we bring into our space. Many single folks are selective about a potential Mr. Right or Ms. Perfect; nonetheless, they are ready to share their lives and freedom. Singles looking for long-lasting relationships turn over every stone in their quest for the right and perfect someone, evidence that folks are serious about their willingness to connect. Once we've learned to love our Self in its entirety—our body, mind, and spirit—it becomes much easier to love the ones we bring in to share our personal space. So far, we surrendered in ways we never thought possible. We accept our life as a journey, we acknowledge our brothers and sisters as companions on the same path, and we are ever mindful of God's faithfulness.

Should it not be a natural progression that we trust God to direct and guide us to the right and perfect someone? The answer, in my opinion, is yes. God puts people together to learn and grow so that they may complete their incompleteness so that they may suspend judgments and, in the end, accept each other as seekers of true love. Some people believe that the perfect someone will take away their fear, guilt, and the negative mishmash they collect and store in their life. Folks have to think that love could walk into their space at any moment and surprise them. Folks could be about their business, unaware that love was observing, and love deliberately walked over and said hello—a hello that sounded different from the ones they'd heard in the past. And love could appear looking different from what (who) folks had in their mind. Know that love is perfect in any form it shows up. I admit that love without conditions is not always a cure for some folks because the more love without conditions; some people get, the more they crave. I completed decades of marriage to understand that the conditions I placed on my love for my husband were not valid. It was not my duty to change and fix my husband into conforming to what I would like him to be. I realized that I needed to be fixed because I am genuinely committed to a lifetime relationship with him. The ones you're with are likely your spouse, family, relatives, folks you form extended partnerships with, and folks you spend eight hours with each day in business relationships. The ones you're with are folks you are obliged to accept in the way they were presented to you. They don't have to reciprocate love, and they may not want to be with you all of the time—love them anyway. When you completely accept and love the ones you're with, you radiate more love. You know you're in sync with your world, and you are worthy of love in return.

Love is all about you

Love is the way you respond to others; love is saying: *I love you*, to someone you truly admire, love is fun and laughter, love is your smile, love is your warmth, the sound of your voice, the touch of your hand, love is celebrating a special day with someone, love is giving, love is showing kindness. Love is all about you—love is true Self in motion. Let us talk about love as a minimum requirement. I am talking about a simple *hello* and *thank-you*. When someone says hello, we know we should acknowledge the compliment. But love gets uncertain for many because they are afraid to give the minimum measure to people they do not know or may never see again. Many people are scared to accept a loving gesture because of the strings they attach. Everyone is in love with the next person—we do not recognize this fact. Yes, I know about evil, hate, jealousy, war, and so on, but those are demonstrations of love turned inside out and upside down. People and situations will sometimes tick us off. Some people will make it their duty to cause us grief and pain; they will deliberately test our commitment to love. They will do and say things to make us question the love we give. Many times I have had to address situations and people who tested my faith and bruised my spirit. Those situations kicked me in the shins and knocked me down. But instead of saying, *look at what she has done to me*? I say, *look what love has done*.

In the middle of whatever is happening to you, try not to fall out of love. Love is stronger than the Egos of other people. It is not about their love for you; it is about your love for them!

Love is all about *you*
Love is your smile
Love is fun and laughter
Love is hello and thank-you
Love is the name we call our spouse
Love is the name we call our children
Love is our connection to the love of others
Love is the reason we forgive ourselves
Love is how we know there are no judgments

Loving Memories

I am quick to encourage folks to cherish their memories, for memories are what they carry to the end—even though I am first to admit that some memories are burdens to be cast off and be rid of—all of us have memories we'd prefer to lose. People hold on to memories and reference them as happy or not so happy. A past love relationship that did not serve you well might not have been all that bad—life will give folks practical situations to learn from. I say love should be enjoyed while it serves you because life could require you to surrender your *love experience* at any time. Try not to hold on to relationships that already served the time to prolong a worn-out sensation because you could experience the unbearable pain of rejection. People enter our lives for a season and, without a doubt, for a reason. Sometimes we never found out the real reason. However, we should relish the season.

Promises validate our credibility

I promised myself to be responsible for my negative thoughts, words, feelings, irrational behaviors, and foolish actions. Ultimately owning my unwanted *stuff* allows me to ask for forgiveness. When we make a promise, we give our word. We guarantee delivery, and we put our integrity on the line. Our promises validate our credibility and assure others that we can be trusted. People will make promises, then break them when a different or an unforeseen situation pops up. False promises, broken promises, and overdue promises often disappoint other people. There will indeed be times when folks make promises in good faith, but because of different circumstances that were not obvious at that moment, the promises were not kept. I suggest that folks own up to the broken trust and ask to be forgiven in situations where they have to break a promise. And if the contract becomes overdue, they should ask to be understood and re-negotiate a new delivery as quickly as possible. Most people recognize the degree to which they can extend promises that genuinely support their commitments, and they usually try to deliver on those promises. Honor your promises. Don't be embarrassed to own so-called failures and deficiencies that may arise due to a promise you made. Know that most obligations and assurances are negotiable.

Grace is amazing

It was Grace that taught my heart to fear and Grace my fears relieved / How precious did that Grace appears, the hour I first believed. —John Newton, "*Amazing Grace*"

Grace is God's unconditional love on display in every living thing. Grace was present at conception, Grace is the breath of life, Grace is our beating heart, Grace brought us to this point on our journey through life, Grace is continuous flow of all good things, Grace moves without effort—Grace is amazing!

Grace will appear in our life as elegance, sophistication, and beauty. Grace as beauty is style, having a healthy glow, and commanding admiration. Grace, as love is what we give without counting the cost! "*The Grace of our Lord Jesus Christ be with you all.*" *1 Thess. 5:8.*

The preceding Grace declaration assures our faith and reminds us of God's unconditional love. Grace is mercy!

The famous song "*Amazing Grace.*" is one that warms my heart. That song envelops me with comforting feelings every time I hear it. "How precious did that Grace appear, the hour I first believed." —John Newton, "*Amazing Grace.*"

Use acceptable words

"Talk in everlasting words, and dedicate them all to me/
And I will give you all my life/ I'm here if you should call to me/ You think that I don't even mean a single word I say/ It's only words, and words are all I have, to take your heart away."
—The Bee Gees, "*Words*"
Let the words of my mouth and the meditation of my heart be acceptable in thy sight, O Lord my strength and my redeemer.
—Psalms 19:14

Words are our thoughts revealed; words are our heart's spoken desires; words are our feelings laid bare; words are for learning. Without words, we would not be able to put into action our desires or aid in the desires of other people, for that matter. Words signify power whether spoken or written. The dilemma with words is that when emphasis is placed on them in certain ways, they carry different and, perhaps, unintended meanings. Individuals might disapprove or be offended by some words' meaning and might see those words as criticisms. Words such as *you are ugly, you are fat, you are a loser, you will amount to nothing, lazy*, and *how could you be so stupid*; are out of bounds for many people. Don't rebuke Self with unloving words or use unloving words to admonish others. Positive words are ideal. Use acceptable words. The phrase, "Sticks and stones may break my bones, but words will not hurt me," does not work for everyone. People show respect by expressing thoughtful words when they dialogue. Words may be all you have to give; however, your thoughtful words may be the only encouraging statement that someone else heard in a long time. Words are plenty; they are powerful; give words with love.

PART FOUR:

ALL IS WELL

It is possible that the thing you spent the central part of your life doing was not your purpose in life. Know that life will stop you in your tracks and turn you around to make you pay attention to your purpose—your purpose is the thing you've been sidestepping, the thing you know in your heart you were called to do.

Great is Thy Faithfulness

I LOVE TO SING the *Thank You* song. I tap my feet to the words as I sit in quiet contemplation, I hum the tune softly during meditation, and quite often, I recite the lines as a prayer. Most people have words and verses that they recite during reflective moments. What are your favorite melodies? Do you sing them often? Do they satisfy you spiritually?

> *Thank you for waking me this morning*
> *Thank you for giving me today*
> *Thank you for e'ery new day dawning*
> *I'll be thanking you.*
> —*Jack Fishman/Marty Schneider*

We have discussed scenarios, dealt with Self and Ego, love and fear, and we have met and addressed many of our ups and downs. We've made bold changes in areas that were hitherto off-limits. We can honestly say all is well. All is well because we recognize we are headed for a peaceful conclusion to our journey through life. We know that our path is aligned with our real purpose, so we are less likely to be knocked off our course. All is well because our Built-in Prayer Mechanism is within, waiting to be called up. As we journey, let's accept other travelers as participants in this life mission, although some people may be moving faster or slower or taking different routes.

...and our purpose, does purpose matter?

People will say they have a specific life purpose, but not everyone will develop their purpose. Why is this? Because some folks might believe their *reason* is their purpose—be it marrying a particular individual or choosing a specific profession. Fortunately for many, they recognized their *purpose* for pursuing a specific path was, in fact, a distraction from their real purpose, and they changed direction. Not many people would turn down a job promotion because they thought it paid more than they deserve or quit a permanent job that provided adequately for their family to take a six-month contract that paid twice as much. All of us have our *reason* for making crucial decisions: Is your *reason* your purpose? Is your focus your purpose? Is your mission your purpose? I say your purpose is much more than your ambition or a specific goal; your purpose is the idea you always wanted to pursue, the notion that kept nudging you, but you were too scared to pursue because of fear of what others might say. The moment you wake up to the thing you love to do, the talent that brings you joy, the skill you work at 24/7 and then give it away with love, you know you've found your real purpose. Carefully think through your ambitions, consider the distractions your Ego may present, listen to your true Self then yield to your purpose. Your purpose is the *thing* your quiet voice within says you can and should do. Your purpose is the idea you always wanted to pursue.

Detach commitments from burdens

Let's separate commitments from burdens. Burdens are things to be cast off; commitments can be re-negotiated. If you are experiencing sleepless nights because of your commitments, if you are tired and lack energy because your obligations make you nervous, if your commitments consume too much of your time, you know it is time to cast off those burdensome commitments on Spirit within and go free. Consider the following, which I call burdens: If your stomach turns when your rent is due, then your monthly payments are burdensome; you may need to re-negotiate those monthly payments. If the lease on your dream car is more than your rent, then you may need to downsize your car. If you've been absent from your job because your dog is sick and your supervisor makes you crazy, then you do not like your job—you may need to pay attention to the idea that keeps nudging you—the *thing* you'd rather be doing, but you fear criticisms from other people.

List the things you possess at this moment—things that make you feel good. What is your commitment to those things? Seriously, what is your commitment? Do those things feel like millstones? Is your commitment to those things validated by your authentic signature? Could you give and take on the things you're committed to for a peaceful and stress-free life? Write down the things you're committed to, ponder them, measure them one against the other, label them good and not-so-good, decide which ones are burdens to cast off. Cast them off and go free. I have committed to other people's responsibilities out of fear. Fear will make folks say *yes* when they meant to say *no*. Don't let your commitments turn into unnecessary burdens because burdens will attack your heart. It is not a bad idea to be committed to things that express prosperity, but does your commitment to those things offer you the certainty of a peaceful and happy life? Are you convinced that you even want to encourage a burdensome obligation? The perfect way out of demanding commitments is to cast off the things that burden you and go free. Give them up. It may not seem like the right thing to do at that moment—nevertheless, trust the Word and "cast your burden upon the Lord" (*Psalms 55:22*). In your moments of worries, when you feel like you are between a rock and a hard place, know that there is no hard place, but there is a rock, and that rock is you. Rely on your Self to show you out of demanding situations take your own advice, access your built-in problem-solving system. Cast off those weighty burdens and commit to things that offer you a peaceful and happy life.

Make your commitments your choice

Most, if not all, of what occurs in our life is based on personal choices. When we think we're not participating, we can be sure that others are making choices for us that may not be to our liking. An unacceptable option suggests that someone else made a judgment. Everyone can and should make choices that benefit them. I get nervous when friends ask me to choose (for example) an eat-in place because I could very well be the only member of the group enjoying the meal if my choice of a restaurant was not right for the group. Choices made on behalf of others may not be to their liking. Be responsible for your own choices. Often people make choices that steer them down a badly-trampled path or engage them in certain activities so that they may learn or teach someone else an unforgettable lesson. All choices, good, bad, forced, or bold, will ultimately affect people's life. Choices make us take ownership of outcomes. Some choices cause anxiety.

The choice of a wife or husband immediately comes to mind. Marsha married a man of a different race and culture. Family and friends expressed dismay. As far as they were concerned, that was the wrong choice. With respect, Marsha and John gave serious thought to all that society said could go wrong in their marriage, yet Marsha and John were prepared to defend their choice. Every time we make and re-make a personal choice, we are genuinely considering other people's right to make their own choices. Most people rely on their moment-by-moment choices to be sensible decisions, but even well thought out moment-by-moment choices should be subject to revisions. People are at liberty to change their minds about prior choices as they wish, and they should be prepared to defend the choices they've made. Folks can and should revisit personal choices that they once doubted and, where appropriate, give opinions, express wishes, and make opposite selections. Your choices give you the upper hand. Know that when you don't choose, you allow others to choose for you. Other people's choices may not be ideal, and when people sense your choices to be wishy-washy, they may dismiss your approach. Be sure that the choices you make are ones that you are prepared to defend. Remember: an unacceptable choice suggests someone else made a judgment; choices you once doubted can and should be revisited.

Choices reflect true Self

Dorothy's husband Eric stayed out late—much too late—with no satisfactory excuse, and often when he came home, he was too tired to engage in family activities. He was tardy with handling household finances, and important commitments were left unattended. Dorothy was nervous and unhappy about her state of affairs. She considered confronting Eric about her troubling observations but perished the thought because of her fear of his anger. She imagined she might be *losing it*. More to the point, she was losing him! Dorothy contemplated some options, taking into account her parental responsibilities to their son Rayon. Number one, to survive a marital shake-up, she would need additional financial assistance. Number two, their son Rayon would surely be adversely affected by any move that split the family, and, number three, how in the world was she going to face the onslaught of criticisms and judgments once the word got out about a split in her family? Eric never gave a split in the family the same measured thought—the split happened. Some folks are slow to recognize that their choice was not ideal for their specific challenge, and subsequent decisions or other choices regarding the same matter might not be best. This was true for Dorothy and Eric when they opted for a divorce. Choices that do not turn out to your satisfaction can and should be revisited. It would help if you reconsidered personal choices and express new wishes. When you don't choose, you allow other people to choose for you.

Give and take, wiggle room—does it matter?

Every day, folks make personal choices, commit to morals, stand up for principles, *give and take* and find a middle ground. As a consequence, folks find themselves in situations that leave too much wiggle room. I often hear: How much *give and take* is enough, and where is the middle ground? My answer is, we ought to give and take as much as is needed, and; we know we've reached the middle ground when we've given more than we've taken. Consider Gino, for example. Gino's job did not pay as much as his wife Angie's, so Angie handled the major household bills. Their three school-aged children required more looking-after as they grew older. Angie struggled to keep up. Gino often reminded Angie that he was already paying the property taxes on their home and could not commit to additional household bills. And, anyway, the monthly payments on his truck, his motorbike, and his stereo system absorbed the rest of his paycheck. The household expenses became considerably less for Gino and Angie when their children grew up and left home. Still, Gino maintained that it was Angie's responsibility to carry on with handling major household bills. Don't be on the left side of a middle ground, don't give more than you are allowed to take, move out of gray areas, review your wiggle room, and re-negotiate your flexibility.

Forgiveness is the way forward

I am a mall-walker. Mall-walkers are folks who do walking exercises inside of their neighborhood malls before the malls open for business. At the end of an hour of walk, I would go into the food court to have a coffee. On one of my coffee stops, I struck up a conversation with a fellow mall walker. The conversation turned to the subject of forgiveness. She was having a difficult time forgiving a fellow life traveler. Without hesitation, she told me of misdeeds and wrongs the individual had done to her and how she felt responsible for forgiving and bringing closure to the matter. I admit I am not the one to advise about forgiveness, for I have had some vengeful feelings about people I believed to have done me wrongs, which I never could determine—meaning I was angry at folks for no good reason. So I said to my colleague, "Forgive *you* first." At that very moment, I knew I misspoke because she soundly admonished me for implying she was a participant in whatever the wrong had been. She was right; she should accept no blame. No one needs to accept blame. No one is right or wrong; everyone and everything is the way it *is*. Here are a few realities about taking responsibility for Self that folks ought to take seriously. If you're out of cash, overweight, holding on to a dead-end job, and you need to see the dentist, it is time to forgive *you* for allowing your Self to deteriorate. If you blame yourself for their foolishness, forgive *you* because you are not responsible for their stupidity. If you think that someone or something can hinder you from manifesting your true potential—forgive *you* because no one can hinder your progress. If you think religion, politics, world affairs, and the dog are making you unhappy—forgive *you*. Always remember, you decide your happiness. When you forgive, you're acknowledging that you're ready to be responsible for Self, prepared to switch gears, prepared to make a fresh start, ready for the next steps. You express that you have cleansed yourself of the dirt that other people heaped on you, and you're ready to move on. Do remember: nothing is right or wrong about how you forgive; forgiveness clears the way forward, heals broken hearts, and gives folks another chance. Forgiveness is best for our overall health.

Starting over

"Starting all over again is gonna be rough, so rough/But we gonna make it/Starting all over as friends is gonna be rough on us/But we gotta face it."
—Hall and Oates, *Starting All Over Again*

I wished someone had advised me to learn from my mistakes and begin again. Having this information would have helped me to move through some of my difficult lessons quickly. People who live public lives have a much harder time correcting apparent mistakes or even starting over. Criticisms of them are more extreme, and opportunities to re-group might be fewer. I encourage folks to make bold attempts. Bold attempts show one's sincerity and seriousness. Brave attempts don't always end with winners—some people have lost. Understand that so-called losses are new ways to learn and additional chances to try again. There is never a good reason not to start over. When the thought of starting over enters your mind, don't shun the idea. It is possible that the thing you spent the major part of your life doing might not be your purpose, know that life could turn you around and make you acknowledge your real purpose. I entered my mid-fifties, having progressed through a healthy, prosperous life. Then, to my amazement, life turned me around and pointed me in a new direction on an unfamiliar path. Spirit revealed to me that the difficulties I experienced were not different from other people's problems. The prayers that sustained me during those challenging moments—no matter that they were hostile and self-centered—could be inspirational to other people. I wrote my first publication: *And When We Pray*. You may balk at the idea when life turns you around and starts you over; you may kick and scream at the thought of doing something new and different, but in the end, the right thing to do is to start over. Folks should know that every waking moment of their life is an opportunity to begin again and a chance to succeed. Remember this: there is never a good reason not to start over; every waking moment is a new break, be bold; boldness tells others you approached without fear. Also, remember, mistakes were meant to be made; make lots of them, if you will, learn from your mistakes, start afresh!

Why not me?

In the same breath that we ask, *why me?* we should also ask *why not me?* "Why me?" is a question we ask when we believe we've been given a challenging task or a heavy burden. Or when we're faced with a responsibility that we think would be better handled by someone else. In response to suffering or a negative occurrence, we may say, "I never thought this would happen to me." Well, who would be more appropriate? Some of us are masochistic in the way we approach our perceived injustices. Maintaining an unpredictable situation against all odds to stabilize it may not be the perfect solution. A firm and unyielding stance with no plans to adjust, believing that we can ride out a crisis is unwise. Joanne's entire family was impacted by the financial challenges that developed after a negative family choice—a situation that was not the fault of any family member.

However, the blame had to be placed somewhere, and since no one would own the unfavorable outcome, the universe lay the responsibility in the lap of Joanne. She was held responsible for the family business's collapse, the loss of the family's assets, and the fallout from everything that did not go right during the family's turmoil. Joanne's husband refused to accept that the family's loss was as devastating for the other members of his family as it had been for him. He was like a raging bull, relentless in dishing out blame, unforgiving to the point of separating from Joanne. Joanne refused to accept her husband's decision to give up on their marriage; she persevered and, to her delight, her husband reunited with her. You've heard about or have experienced a family crisis that rocked the family at its core and how difficult it was to "hang in there" and watched the situation as it gets worse. Vince and Jackie were distraught over the sudden death of their son and became estranged in their home. Fortunately for Vince and Jackie, they hung in there long enough to heal their broken hearts and subsequently reunited.

The *Why not me* people

You handle complicated matters; you survive touchy situations; you appreciate boundaries; you get along with other people; you respect their right to move at their pace; you survive to tell about it because you asked *why not me*? You are one of the *Why, not me*, people who take action; you ask: *If not me, then who*?

Your Will

I am not referring to the last wishes of an individual. I am talking about your determination, your motivation, your drive, your willpower, your spirit. These are drivers that give folks the impetus to carry on regardless of the circumstances they may be experiencing at the moment. Your will pushes you to do what you know you must do without fear. People usually know what to do to resolve a conflict, but they're unwilling to do it. Why? Fear of being criticized, fear of being wrong, fear of disapproval, fear of loss of love. Fear is the reason folks resist the strength of their will. Fear is always lurking. But people should not allow fear to devour them because situations change, moment to moment—it all depends on how they view life; nothing remains the same.

My friend Helen has been ailing from cancer for a long time. She will tell you that she would rather not wake up some days than to endure another day of excruciating pain. But Helen *accepted* her cancer diagnosis and then proceeded with treatment to cure the disease. She sometimes asks, the *Why me*? Question. I often tell Helen that she is alive to complete an important life assignment despite her misgivings. I remind Helen of how much I learn every time I watch her undergo cancer treatment. I praise her for dutifully carrying out her teaching assignment, and I tell her God will wake her up every morning, as many mornings as are necessary, so that she may teach folks who need to learn the lessons she is assigned to teach, through her battle with cancer. Helen will tell you her motivation for waking up is her commitment to her dependent son's care. Her *will* is to see him *past the worse (*meaning the young man is at a stage in his life where he can take care of himself). In Helen's eyes, her son may not *pass the worse,* but Helen's *will* is enough to make her survive for her son's sake.

On the other hand, my guy-friend Eric concluded another unhealthy love relationship, wasted no time, and quickly entered into a new liaison. But as soon as he entered the new relationship, it screeched to an unhappy ending. Eric laments over his bad luck and vows he would look the other way when he saw a woman. I don't have the answer to Eric's *Why me?*

Why be depressed?

I promised myself many years ago that I would never use the word *depressed* to describe my state of mind unless clinically diagnosed as such. Folks should be sure before they agree they are depressed. For many people, being depressed is an illness that requires therapy; however, there may be depressive conditions that should be diagnosed as temper tantrums. Temper tantrums are fits of anger, loss of reason, inappropriate outbursts, and extended irrationality periods. In many cases, those who *throw* tantrums did not get what they ask for; perhaps a brother who yielded his happiness to someone else; a sister who experienced an unpleasant conclusion or misunderstood. When negative enemy thoughts plunge me into unpleasant situations, I tell myself I am "sad." How is being "sad" different from having a temper tantrum? I am sad because I am dealing with an *uncalled-for* temper tantrum. At that moment, my Ego was encouraging me to be unloving to my Self; Ego made me use unflattering words to describe myself to control my thinking. Phrases like: *I can't, I am messed up, I am an idiot, I am foolish, I will never make it, nobody loves me*, or *I am doomed* are encouraged by Ego to draw attention to Self in a negative way. Temper tantrums may be funny to the onlooker noticing a screaming three-year-old in a toy store at the mall, but the scene may not be so cute to the parent, trying desperately to calm the child. A friend told me she stayed away from work for a week during the company's peak labor period, without prior approval from her boss, because she was too *depressed* to work. I asked her what caused her temper tantrum; she said the company declined her request for her vacation to start on a specific date, which made her unhappy. (By the way, she was annoyed at me that I labeled her retaliation a temper tantrum). Folks should know temper tantrums are real fears showing up inappropriately as revenge. Those who lashed out because they did not get what they wanted or got *even* because they suspected an injustice are accommodating an uncalled-for temper tantrum. If your obvious annoyance doesn't match your charming words, you know you are experiencing a temper tantrum, and you are probably acting up. Without a doubt, other people will notice your inconsistencies and use the observation to their advantage. Do not allow an unsuitable reaction to discredit you. Do remember temper tantrums are fear-based and should be banished into nothingness where they belong.

No reason to freak-out

Those who believe they ought to control their affairs or be the captain of their ship will leave nothing to chance, and if they think they're failing in their effort to handle a situation, they will freak-out or melt down, as the case may be. Folks freak-out because they are worried. I freak-out when I suspect that my plans will not come together the way I planned. Folks who freak-out regularly are expressing an Ego that will present more things to freak-out over. The ego uses freak-outs to consume and make folks unhappy—banish a situation that freaks you out, send the situation into nothingness where it belongs. What would be your reason for a meltdown? Is your reason based on fear, anger, resentment, jealousy, hateful feelings? Is your reason a specific recurring situation? A situation that just keeps ticking you off? A situation that makes you feel unhappy? A situation that did not turn out, right? Did someone rub you the wrong way? If your situation did not turn out to your liking, know that there is absolutely no reason to freak out, get a second opinion, wait for another occasion, find a new way, look for a different reason, start over—a meltdown should be a last resort. Do remember, fear is the chief reason for a breakdown, and fear will show up in many ways, wearing different masks and causing folks to freak-out. Fear keeps folks in control and makes folks meltdown for no good reason.

Dear God
I stand in Your presence covered in dirt
My eyes are filled with dust from my own folly
I cannot see my way out of this mess
I cannot remember how I got this dirt on me
Shake me loose and stand me up
Guide me through this valley
Help me to grasp and understand my lessons
And make me glad once more
In Jesus' name, I pray.
(And When We Pray)

Go with what is flowing at the moment

I tell folks to go with the flow, and I sometimes get rebuked for making such a statement. It is true; people will go with the flow if they like what is flowing. Going with the flow sometimes means you are standing still, holding on to an imaginary tied knot and waiting for divine directions. It means the bigger picture has yet to appear. The flow was not going with Dorothy—her son Rayon was in jail, and she must inform ex-husband Eric about the situation. After their divorce, Dorothy said "*No*" to Eric concerning nurturing decisions on behalf of Rayon, although Eric wanted the family to stay connected. In the end, Eric and Dorothy united along decision-making lines to plan a way forward for their son Rayon.

The Serenity Prayer

God grant me the serenity
to accept the things I cannot change
courage to change the things I can
and wisdom to know the difference
Trusting that He will make all things right
if I surrender to His Will
That I may be reasonably happy in this life
—Reinhold Niebuhr

What is it that's occurring to make you unhappy?

Happiness is different things to different people/That's what happiness is—Annie Moyers

Environments, family, upbringing, schooling, and incidences past and present influence how folks relate and how happy and contented they are about what is happening in their moment. Some people's imaginations may sometimes run amok, and anxiety will develop into situations that overwhelm them and cause unhappiness. Folks should know that life is not static; people are happy and unhappy simultaneously. What is it that is occurring in your life to make you not happy? Are you recovering from a messy divorce? Have you been single for a long time? Did you lose a loved one to death? Do you not feel healthy? Are you just not happy and don't know why? The situation you face may be hurtful and uncomfortable but know that there is always something you can do about how you feel. To make a change, you must decide that you want to change the thought, the feeling, the situation, and what makes you unhappy, then proceed with the change. Recall the time when a new relationship snapped you out of a period of prolonged unhappiness, the joy you felt when you discovered that you were expecting a baby and how happy you were when you received a negative result from the test you did at the clinic? Think about those things and be happy. For many, just to wake up to a new day, to be with loved ones is enough happiness. Pain and suffering are major causes of unhappiness. It is unfair to ask someone to be happy when he or she is feeling pain.

I agree that pain and painful situations are challenging to endure, but suffering, on the other hand, is usually an unnecessary choice. Choose not to suffer. Some things that made you unhappy one moment could make you happy the next moment; for example, you could find the job you had been searching for, you could mend the relationship that broke your heart, and your lost wallet with everything intact could be found and returned to you. During periods of so-called unhappiness, folks should consider adapting to happy activities that may be happening at the moment. If a friend celebrates a child's birth or a grandchild, commemorate the occasion with that friend. Your happiness is nobody's business. You decide what makes you happy, you call the shots, and you savor your happy moments. Loving relationships, bouquets, sweet chocolates are things that make everyone happy; give yourself a happiness break!

PART FIVE:

OUR FAITHFULNESS

Individuals make pledges and declarations, take oaths and vows, and present trophies, certificates, bands of significance, and gifts to show their faithfulness in significant ways, and the grades and value they assign to their faithfulness indicate their level of genuineness and authenticity.

Great is Thy Faithfulness

HOW GREAT IS your faithfulness? Are you faithful in your pledges? Firm in your declarations? Dependable and truthful? Can your faithfulness be trusted? In a real way, our faithfulness should be flawless assurances; unvarnished genuineness, perfect and unembellished rightness. But how many individuals can live up to such authenticity? Individuals make pledges and declarations, take oaths and vows, and present trophies, certificates, bands of significance, and gifts to show their faithfulness in significant ways, and the grades and value they assign to their faithfulness indicate their level of genuineness and authenticity. How great is your faithfulness? You are assured of God's faithfulness; how great is your faithfulness to Him? Have you been faithful in worship, faithful in praise, faithful in adoration, and faithful in thanksgiving? Do you regularly give thanks for the things you take for granted—your beating heart and the breaths you take, the earth and its many gifts, the waters that sustain your existence, and the people around you who are kind and loving—did you thank God for putting those people in your space? Did you thank Him for your wake-up call this morning? Your faithfulness is the honesty with which you show your love; it is the truth that others can rely on; it is the things you do that show you're real; your faithfulness is revealed in what you give (not what you take); your faithfulness is your reliance on divine Spirit to supply all that you need.

Expressions of our faithfulness

We express faithfulness to the waiter in a restaurant and the attendant at the petrol station by giving regular tips, and yet we forget to be faithful to Self. We guarantee faithfulness to people we're familiar with by making vows, declarations, oaths, and pledges. However, we caution that vows can be broken, nuptials can end in divorces, and deals may be scrapped. Is it any wonder that some folks find it challenging to accept that faithfulness is new every morning?

It is of the Lord's mercies that we are not consumed because his compassions fail not. They are new every morning: Great is thy faithfulness. (Lamentations 8:22-23)

Dorothy was sad. Family and friends judged her divorce from Eric as faithfulness turned upside down. She was weary from the shame of her son's incarceration, and living single was a real challenge for her. Dorothy stayed in the *valley* of faithfulness for a very long time, continually picking up the pieces of her life and often putting them back in places where they don't fit. She remained in her *valley* to observe the value and grades of faithfulness and learn to rely on Self. If folks don't experience faithfulness to their liking, they might express disappointments. Folks might feel *let down* when their hard work did not pay off. I felt *let down* when my prayers for relief were not answered to my satisfaction. People experienced *letdowns* when something did not happen for them, but there is no need to feel *let down* or believe your worth is *less*. *Letdowns* are the games Ego play to bring relevancy to itself. Know that you are created to live happy, healthy, and whole, divine Spirit within assures you of faithfulness to Self and, in due course, draws to you the faithfulness of other folks.

You and I have come a long way

You now know that Self needs to be attended to, and you're ready to do new things for Self. You're eager to go boldly towards your purpose—the thing that pops up in your mind, but you push it back every time because you fear what other people might say. You believe your Built-in Prayer Mechanism will direct you as you move forward prayerfully, but there is an amount of hesitation—you're afraid you may let Self down. I will tell you right now; you will not let Self down. A moment in time will come when all of us, you and I, will seriously survey the path we've been traveling. That's the moment when life calls on us to *take stock*, reassess, if you will, the destination we chart. It is a point where we look around—see how far we've come and how much time we have remaining to get where we need to be. At that point, we determine whether the conditions under which we had been traveling still satisfy our continuing journey. Some of us may decide we might be better served to stay the course; even though we may be dissatisfied with our progress, the courageous folks will take bold steps and make brave changes. Some folks will say they were napping as time passes—I say, touché. Living is a process that involves participation, and it is unlikely that anyone would be *napping* while time is passing. The truth is some folks are far too preoccupied with the issues in their life to notice that the treadmill on which they've been walking is moving too fast.

Where did the time go?

The question folks ask after they take stock of their life and realize that nothing significant happens for them in a long time, although they recognize that big and important things generally happen. For example, their children became graduates, one or two of them married, grandchildren arrived, relatives and friends passed on, innovations and devices came on the scene—a realization that time did not stand still! With an amount of sadness, some folks will declare they missed out on a phase of their life; I say every moment is an opportunity to start again, every phase is a new beginning—start over, it is never too late. It might be time to do a new thing—do as Spirit leads. If things did not turn out as planned in one phase of your life, it might not have been the right time—yet. Folks are beginning to examine Self in a big way. Spirit within is shifting to the revival of souls.

"Stand/ There's a cross for you to bear/ Things to go through if you're going anywhere/ Stand/ For the things you know are right/ It's the truth that the truth makes them so uptight/ Stand/ All the things you want are real/ You have you to complete, and there is no deal/ Stand."
—Sly and the Family Stone, *Stand!*

With love from me to you

Thank you for journeying along with me thus far. I feel honored to write this book and present it to you in these few words. I shared some experiences about my own spiritual journey that I felt might encourage you to choose the loving traits of Self over the selfish characteristics of Ego. I told you that my journey was not different from yours. We experience many of the same challenges; we pray together, trust together, we are all children of God. I hope you recognized that my words came from the core of which I am, the heart of my being. I am truly grateful that you've come to this page. The thought that I might engage you to this point made it possible for me to be my authentic Self as I delivered my message. You may think I said a lot, although I know I've said too little. I hope you were inspired by some of what I've written. My purpose was to read and arrive at your pivotal moments— moments when you recognized your own truth. I hope you stopped to savor those moments, and if you were made stronger, then I am pleased. You may have found some of my admissions entertaining or perhaps witty or, you may have raised your hand and said yes to examples I gave. Whatever the impact, I hope some of my insights got stuck in your memory. You are correct to say nothing is ever final, and everything is subject to change. However, you should know that change is your responsibility. Your journey should not lead you to *who knows where, who knows when*. Your journey begins in your heart and ends in the heart of your fellowman. As you look to the future and consider the way forward, I hope you will reflect on the things that stuck in your psyche. Please consider the following suggestions:

Suggestion #1—Recognize the behavior of Ego

Ego's plan is to divide and conquer. Ego is insecure; it is in love with itself. The ego will appear in different forms and sizes, wearing different masks to deceive. If you are not feeling *the* love, then Ego is raising its ugly head; banish Ego into nothingness where it belongs. Refuse to accommodate an uncalled-for Ego when it shows up.

Suggestion #2—Do not give in to Ego

Do not give in to Ego as it struggles to cope with life issues; treat Ego with love. Tell Ego its plan to divide and conquer, and have its own way, is no longer relevant because love just walked in.

Suggestion #3—Tame Ego with love

Ego's desire to maintain its influence over the true Self will subside when Self shows Ego how to love. Tame Ego with love so that Ego and its many masks will recoil and be born again/born anew to love.

Suggestion #4—Love Self

Love is who you are. Your love is your smile, your love is warm to touch, your love is fun and laughter, your love says hello and thank-you, your love shows in everything you do, your love connects you to the love of others, your love is without judgment, and your love is all about you.

Suggestion #5—Self is your nature

Self is your true nature, your character, your spirit. Self seeks to replace Ego with love; Self will not accommodate other people's inconsiderate judgments. Self is the love side of your Ego. Ego says, do it now. Self says, wait a moment. Be merciful to Self. The term Self-propelled takes on a new meaning when you recognize that everything about you is appointed for your good—everything is as it should be. Self is your best ally.

Suggestion #6—Fear not

Fear will creep up on you when you're not paying attention. Fear is a liar; refuse to believe the lies fear tells. Most of the things you fear will likely not happen; the lies fear tell will confuse your mind and make you believe untruths. Be ready to address the fear that confronts and defeat it. Drive out fear in whatever form it shows up. Fear not.

Suggestion #7—Be authentic

Authenticity is the truth. You decide how you will show up. Will you be authentic or will you be hidden behind a fear mask of your choosing? Speak truth to Self and other people. Be who you are because you can be no one else. Authenticity allows you to be, without being.

Suggestion #8—Your Faithfulness

Faithfulness is showing you are real; it is your gift of love. Faithfulness is your perfect and unembellished rightness, your confidence in the divine Spirit within.

Suggestion #9—Believe—all things are possible

Have faith—believe. Believe in your capabilities. Approach the throne of Grace boldly. There are no mistakes, only lessons to be learned. Believe—all things are possible.

Great is Thy Faithfulness

Suggestion #10—Draw on your Built-in Prayer Mechanism
Your Built-in Prayer Mechanism is otherwise called your Comforter; it stirs your faith and informs you of everything you need to know when you need to know. Your Built-in Prayer Mechanism is that peaceful surge of wind that lifts your spirit and reminds you that God your Provider is in your midst. Yield to your Built-in Prayer Mechanism when you pray.

Suggestion #11—Pray always
Your prayers are your conversations with God and your spiritual connection with like-minded praying folks. Put your trust, confidence, and reliance on the awesome power of your prayers. Pray always.

Suggestion #12—Be Grateful
Be grateful for health, family, and friends. Be grateful for life and blessings. Be grateful for gifts, large and small. Be grateful to God, the Giver, and the Gift.

Suggestion #13—Surrender
Surrender means to give way, let go and let God into your challenging situations. In other words, cast off anything that burdens you. Don't be discouraged because you surrendered—know that you already have everything you need to survive life's journey.

Suggestion #14—Commit to it

Ask yourself these questions:
> Have I been faithful in love?
> Have I been faithful to Self?
> Have I been faithful to people's trust?
> Am I committed to my faithful deeds?
> Do I treat others with respect?
> How will I show up?

Suggestion #15—Own up
Own your emotions: loving feelings, happiness, fear, anger, resentment, jealousy—own them all, then reject the ones you don't want.

Suggestion #16—Be aware
Pay attention to what is going on in your life. Everything that happens to you carries with it a call for action. Give attention to what is manifesting.

Suggestion #17—Build and maintain healthy relationships
Your journey connects you with people and relationships for a reason and perhaps for a reason. Savor the reason and let go when the season is ended. Do not hold on to a relationship to re-live a sensation.

Suggestion #18—Respect Self and others

Respect for Self draws the respect of other people to you. Show respect for other people's boundaries, traditions, languages, their right to worship in their own way, and their right to be different. Respect comes easier when you see other folks as travelers on the same path.

Suggestion #19—Forgive-move pass hurtful feelings

Forgive bad words and deeds that other people pile up on you. Forgive yourself for every thought, word, and deed that keeps you from realizing your potential. Move beyond hurtful feelings. You forgive because you're ready to move forward.

Suggestion #20—Watch your words

Words may be all you have to give; your thoughtful words may be the only encouraging statement that someone else heard in a long time. Give words with love.

Suggestion #21—Mind your own business

Your spiritual journey is your *business*. Your responsibility is to your *business;* take care of your own *business*. Tread carefully around other people's *business* for other people's *business* could hinder your progress and hold you back.

Suggestion #22—Stand - You have you to complete

It might be time to express a new point of view—say and do as true Self directs. If things did not turn out as planned in one phase of your life, it might not have been the right time—yet. Stand for your core beliefs, the things you know are right. Stand and be what you want to be, stand because others are watching you, stand and be relevant.

Suggestion #23

"All the things you want are real/You have you to complete, and there is no deal/Stand."

—Sly and the Family Stone, *Stand!*

PRAYERS

Matthew 6: 9-13

Our father which art in heaven
Hallowed be thy name
Thy kingdom come, thy will be done on earth
as it is in heaven
Give us this day our daily bread
And forgive us our debts, as we forgive our debtors
And lead us not into temptation, but deliver us from evil
For thine is the kingdom and the power and the glory forever
and ever
Amen.

Prayer of St. Francis of Assisi

Lord make me an instrument of Your peace;
Where there is hatred, let me sow love;
Where there is injury, pardon;
Where there is error, the truth;
Where there is doubt, the faith;
Where there is despair, hope;
Where there is darkness, light;
Where there is sadness, joy;
O Divine Master; Grant that I may not so much seek
To be consoled, as to console;
To be understood, as to understand;
To be loved, as to love;
For it is in giving that we receive;
It is in pardoning that we are pardoned.

The Serenity Prayer

God grant me the serenity

to accept the things I cannot change;

courage to change the things I can;

and wisdom to know the difference

Living one day at a time;

Enjoying one moment at a time;

Accepting hardships as the pathway to peace;

Taking, as He did, this sinful world

as it is, not as I would have it;

Trusting that He will make all things right

if I surrender to His Will;

That I may be reasonably happy in this life

and supremely happy with Him

Forever in the next

Amen.

—Reinhold Niebuhr

Prayers from: And When We Pray
(by Olive Rose Steele)
God, our Heavenly Father
We give You thanks for this moment
Your sons and daughters have come together in love
For a meeting of our hearts and minds
Bind us in perfect harmony
Show us Your plan for our lives
Let everything we say and do be to Your
Honor and glory
We love You; We adore You
We honor Your presence
We sing praises to You
We thank You for Your goodness
At this moment of shared friendship and respect
Bless us all and grant us Your peace
"Behold how good and how pleasant it is for
Brethren to dwell together in unity" (Psalms 133:1)
Amen.

Great is Thy Faithfulness

Dear God

Lord and Father of all

Teach me to be respectful of others

To be respectful of their traditions

To be respectful of their worship and praise

To be respectful of their language

To be respectful of their right to be different

To be respectful of Your Divine Spirit

Within each and every one of Your children

Give me an open and loving heart

To love as You love

And help me to be respectful of myself before

I ask others to be respectful of me

In Jesus name, I pray

Amen.

Dear God

Thank You for waking me up this morning

Thank You for giving me today

Thank You for every new day that I see

Thank You for every new sound that I hear

Thank You for the air that I breathe

Thank You for the soft morning dew drops

Thank You for the warm sunlight

Thank You for food, shelter, and clothing

Thank You for family and friends

Thank You for everyone who loves me

Thank You for a healthy, happy life

Thank You that I enjoy these blessings

Father, I am very thankful

Amen.

Great is Thy Faithfulness

Dear God
Direct me to my purpose
Show me to my dreams
Lead me to contentment
Fill me with loving emotions
Comfort me with sacred Songs
Bless me
And grant me the desires of my heart
In Jesus name, I pray
Amen.

Olive Rose Steele

Dear God
I come to You with a heavy heart
I am sad, and I don't know why
Please take away this sadness that's hanging over me
Remove this fear of loneliness that's devouring me
I am depleted
Renew a right Spirit within me
Strengthen me to stand up to the menace of this fear
Father, circle me with love that lifts me up
Put a new song in my heart and
Make me glad again
In Jesus name, I pray
Amen.

Great is Thy Faithfulness

Dear God

I give You the contents of my heart

Purify with fire that which is unclean

Cleanse and use that which is useable

Bless me with a happy, loving, and prosperous life

Enclose me with joy and total bliss

My spirit salutes the holiness in other spirits

My arms reach out in comfort to other arms

Keep me in oneness with my divine purpose

As I remain in Your service

In Jesus name, I pray

Amen.

Dear God
This situation makes me feel helpless
I release my opinions
I relinquish my ideas
I lay down my human will
I put aside my human planning
I give up my human ambitions
I abandon my human pride and vanity
I now give this heavy burden to You, Father
I ask You to adjust and govern this situation
Take full control of the outcome
And bless everyone involved
Amen.

Great is Thy Faithfulness

Dear God

Please protect my mind from lies and enemy thoughts

Help me to hear Your voice over any other clearly

Shield me from misleading and destructive thinking

Where enemy thoughts are already in my mind

Help me to push them back by inviting the power of Your divine Holy Spirit to cleanse my thinking

Protect my thoughts from doubt and confusion

So that I can make right and proper judgments

Have mercy upon me Dear God

In Jesus Name

Amen.

Dear God

Thank you for my friends

My friends have shown me, tremendous love

They support me in good and not-so-good times

They bless me with gifts I would not have asked for

Their love is nourishment in tough times

Father, I appreciate my friends for their generosity

Let me be a source of their happiness

Let me be as good a friend to them as they are to me

Bless their families

Supply their needs

May angels hover and protect all of my friends

And may my friends and I always be together

In Jesus name

Amen.

Great is Thy Faithfulness

Dear God

Have mercy on my mother

She held me in her arms at birth

She nurtured me in my formative years

She gave me advice when I needed

I thank you for directing the role she played in my life

She is on her way to the place You prepared for her

Please give me the strength to support her on her journey

May angels watch over her and comfort her

In Jesus' name, I pray

Amen.

Olive Rose Steele

Dear God
I lift up my friend Helen
And place her on your healing alter
Look favorably upon her
Wrap your protective arms around her
Purify her body of the malignant growth
that makes her sick
Give her more years to complete earthly business
May angels care for her and comfort her
Father, In the name of Jesus Christ
Heal your ailing child and make her whole
Amen.

CLOSING PRAYER AS A SONG

May the good Lord bless and keep you
Whether near or far away
May you find that long-awaited golden day today
May your troubles all be small ones
And your fortunes ten times ten
May the good Lord bless and keep you till
we meet again
May you walk with sunlight shining and a
bluebird in every tree
May there be a silver lining back of every cloud you see
Fill your dreams with sweet tomorrows
Never mind what might have been
May the good Lord bless and keep you till we meet again
(May you walk with sunlight shining) and a bluebird in every
tree... —Meredith Willson, Composer

EPILOGUE

Your first reaction might be, *Great is thy Faithfulness* is another self-help book, and if you believe that it is, you are correct. This book is written to help folks deal with the issues of life that pop up, moment-by-moment, to reassure folks that they're not alone in their worries and to give comfort to folks who believe their issues are insurmountable. Issues and challenges are mostly the same for people of diverse cultures, languages, and beliefs, so this book's contents are pertinent to all. A book such as this one might help those interested in peaceful living, and a recommended read for life travelers with a spiritual mindset. What are peaceful living and a spiritual perspective to an individual who does not reference herself to a doctrine? Should she perceive herself as an unholy outsider relegated to damnation? Everyone should recognize her right to peace, happiness, and wholesome life. I recommend that you embrace the advice within the pages of *Great is thy Faithfulness* and consider the inspiration you will receive from this Edition. If this book is your introduction to an inspirational discourse, I encourage you to seek out similar books as often as possible. I hope that all can begin to be liberated from fears and false notions. People who air their sensibilities are ready like never before to approach life issues, knowing that nothing is the way it seems, and everything is subject to change.

Olive Rose Steele.

PARTING WORDS FROM THE AUTHOR

Has *Great is thy Faithfulness* impacted your life? Has it made a difference in how you see yourself, how you relate to others, how you see your relationship with God? Would you empower others by telling them about *Great is thy Faithfulness?* If so, please help me to help others. Please share the message of *Great is Thy Faithfulness* if it changed your life and set you free. Think about others you know that are still drifting. Share a copy of *Great is thy Faithfulness*. Consider individuals seeking to change their way of living and thinking; present them with a copy. Think about the people you socialize with, work with, and worship with; can you think of someone who needs to experience emotional healing? Spiritual healing? Give them the contact information on how to get a copy of *Great is Thy Faithfulness*. We will make sure a copy of this book gets into their hands as quickly as possible—give the gift of words.

BIBLIOGRAPHY

Farrini, Paul. *Love Without Conditions: Reflections of the Christ Mind*. Greenfield: Heartways Press, 1994.

His Holiness The Dalai Lama. *The Path to Tranquility*. New York: Penguin Books, 1999.

Kuntz, David. *Quiet Mind*. York Beach: Conari Press, 2003.

Walsch, Neale Donald. *When Everything Changes, Change Everything*. Ashland: EmNin Books, 2009.

Williamson, Marianne. *Illuminata*. New York, N.Y. River Head Books, 1995.

ABOUT THE AUTHOR

Writing is, for Olive Rose Steele, a natural ability and a pastime she enjoys. She founded _Let's/Have/Coffee_, an informal connection that promotes and encourages inspiring conversations about life issues in spontaneous settings. She blends faith and spirituality in comprehensible self–healing ways and draws on life experiences to inspire. Olive Rose Steele is the mother of one and grandmother of two. She lives with her husband, Herbert, in Ontario, Canada

BOOKS BY OLIVE ROSE STEELE

And When We Pray:
Suggestions and Prayers for Living in Spirit
ISBN: 978-0-9810723-0-2
5.5" x 8.5" *(13.97 x 21.59 cm)*
Black & White on White paper

The first published work by Olive Rose Steele, *And When We Pray,* is a book of prayers and suggestions on dealing with the challenges of day-to-day living. *And When We Pray* includes many logged prayers from Steele's prayer journal. With honesty, she reveals her faith in prayer and encourages readers to rely on their prayers' awesome power.

WATT TOWN ROAD *(A Memoir)*
6" x 9" (15.24 x 22.86 cm)
Black & White on Cream paper
ISBN-13: 978-1481005647
ISBN-10: 1481005642
Black & White on Cream paper

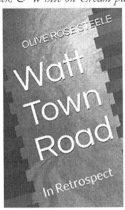

Once again, Olive Rose Steele demonstrates her unique style of expressing the issues of life. WATT TOWN ROAD is a warm and moving journey through the youthful lenses of a young girl growing up in a small, loving, close-knit, and vibrant spiritual community. In the book, the matriarch, Aunty Bea, is a powerful presence. In an unassuming way, she connects and binds the community using her quiet voice and physical space, the kitchen, a place for neighborhood gathering and social reconnecting.

CRY TOUGH
A Novel
ISBN-13:9781072319
Black & White on Cream paper

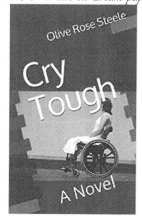

CRY TOUGH is Steele's attempt to link a fictional love story with true-to-life love affairs. Readers will be fascinated by how Steele transitioned from her views on spirit centered thinking to sensuality that mirrors life occurrences.

"In Jamaica, the seasons are the same—sunny days, warm afternoons and cool nights, except those hazy rainy days that make her wish for a new life in a country where spring, summer, fall and winter looks and feels differently. Today, the sun is majestic. There is not a cloud in the blue sky. She stands at the pinnacle of a rock which is molded into the earth by Mother Nature, on a hill overlooking white sands. The ocean breeze is cool and flavorfully salty. She inhales several deep breaths as she surveys the landscape."

Made in the USA
Middletown, DE
09 September 2023

37787130R00104